Performance Assessments for Adult Education

Exploring the Measurement Issues

REPORT OF A WORKSHOP

Committee for the Workshop on Alternatives for Assessing Adult Education and Literacy Programs

Robert J. Mislevy and Kaeli T. Knowles, editors

Board on Testing and Assessment
Center for Education
Division of Behavioral and Social Sciences and Education

NATIONAL ACADEMY PRESS
Washington, DC

NOTICE: The project that is the subject of this report was approved by the Governing Board of the National Research Council, whose members are drawn from the councils of the National Academy of Sciences, the National Academy of Engineering, and the Institute of Medicine. The members of the committee responsible for the report were chosen for their special competences and with regard for appropriate balance.

This study was supported by Contract No. ED-01-CO-0135 between the National Academy of Sciences and the United States Department of Education. Any opinions, findings, conclusions, or recommendations expressed in this report are those of the author(s) and do not necessarily reflect the views of the organizations or agencies that provided support for the project.

International Standard Book Number 0-309-08453-9

Additional copies of this report are available from

National Academy Press
2101 Constitution Avenue, NW
Box 285
Washington, DC 20055
800/624-6242
202/334-3313 (in the Washington Metropolitan Area)
<http://www.nap.edu>

Printed in the United States of America.

Suggested citation: National Research Council. (2002). *Performance assessments for adult education: Exploring the measurement issues, Report of a workshop.* Committee for the Workshop on Alternatives for Assessing Adult Education and Literacy Programs, Robert J. Mislevy and Kaeli T. Knowles, Editors. Board on Testing and Assessment, Center for Education, Division of Behavioral and Social Sciences and Education. Washington, DC: National Academy Press.

THE NATIONAL ACADEMIES

National Academy of Sciences
National Academy of Engineering
Institute of Medicine
National Research Council

The **National Academy of Sciences** is a private, nonprofit, self-perpetuating society of distinguished scholars engaged in scientific and engineering research, dedicated to the furtherance of science and technology and to their use for the general welfare. Upon the authority of the charter granted to it by the Congress in 1863, the Academy has a mandate that requires it to advise the federal government on scientific and technical matters. Dr. Bruce M. Alberts is president of the National Academy of Sciences.

The **National Academy of Engineering** was established in 1964, under the charter of the National Academy of Sciences, as a parallel organization of outstanding engineers. It is autonomous in its administration and in the selection of its members, sharing with the National Academy of Sciences the responsibility for advising the federal government. The National Academy of Engineering also sponsors engineering programs aimed at meeting national needs, encourages education and research, and recognizes the superior achievements of engineers. Dr. Wm. A. Wulf is president of the National Academy of Engineering.

The **Institute of Medicine** was established in 1970 by the National Academy of Sciences to secure the services of eminent members of appropriate professions in the examination of policy matters pertaining to the health of the public. The Institute acts under the responsibility given to the National Academy of Sciences by its congressional charter to be an adviser to the federal government and, upon its own initiative, to identify issues of medical care, research, and education. Dr. Kenneth I. Shine is president of the Institute of Medicine.

The **National Research Council** was organized by the National Academy of Sciences in 1916 to associate the broad community of science and technology with the Academy's purposes of furthering knowledge and advising the federal government. Functioning in accordance with general policies determined by the Academy, the Council has become the principal operating agency of both the National Academy of Sciences and the National Academy of Engineering in providing services to the government, the public, and the scientific and engineering communities. The Council is administered jointly by both Academies and the Institute of Medicine. Dr. Bruce M. Alberts and Dr. Wm. A. Wulf are chairman and vice chairman, respectively, of the National Research Council.

COMMITTEE FOR THE WORKSHOP ON ALTERNATIVES FOR ASSESSING ADULT EDUCATION AND LITERACY PROGRAMS

ROBERT J. MISLEVY (*Chair*), Department of Measurement, Statistics, and Evaluation, University of Maryland, College Park
JUDITH A. ALAMPRESE, Prinicipal Associate, Abt Associates, Bethesda, Maryland
LYLE F. BACHMAN, Department of Applied Linguistics and TESL, University of California, Los Angeles
ROBERT BICKERTON, Adult and Community Learning Services, Massachusetts Department of Education
JOHN P. COMINGS, National Center for the Study of Adult Learning and Literacy, Harvard Graduate School of Education
SUSAN K. COWLES, Instructor, Linn-Benton Community College, Oregon
NEAL SCHMITT, Department of Psychology, Michigan State University
CATHERINE E. SNOW, Graduate School of Education, Harvard University

KAELI T. KNOWLES, *Study Director*
JUDITH A. KOENIG, *Senior Program Officer*
ANDREW E. TOMPKINS, *Senior Project Assistant*

BOARD ON TESTING AND ASSESSMENT

Acknowledgments

At the request of the U.S. Department of Education and the National Institute for Literacy, the National Research Council (NRC) established the Steering Committee for the workshop on Alternatives for Assessing Adult Education and Literacy Programs to examine the development of performance assessments for measuring and reporting learning gains in adult basic education and literacy programs. A great many people contributed to the success of this workshop, which brought together state and local education directors with experts in educational measurement and assessment, and others familiar with the development and implementation of performance assessments. The steering committee would like to thank the speakers and discussants for their contributions in a lively and productive workshop. The full participant list appears in Appendix B.

Staff from the U.S. Department of Education, Office of Vocational and Adult Education (OVAE), under the leadership of Carol D'Amico, and staff from the National Institute for Literacy (NIFL), under the leadership of Andrew Hartman and Sandra Baxter, were valuable sources of information. Ron Pugsley and Mike Dean of OVAE, and Sondra Stein of NIFL were particularly helpful in providing the committee with valuable background information on numerous occasions. Regie Stites of the Stanford Research Institute also provided useful information on Equipped for the Future.

Special thanks are due to a number of individuals at the National Research Council who provided guidance and assistance at many times during the organization of the workshop and the preparation of this report. We thank Pasquale DeVito, director of the Board on Testing and Assessment (BOTA), for his expert guidance and leadership of this project. We are indebted to Judy Koenig for her assistance in planning the workshop and writing this report; she was the principal source of expertise in both the substance and the process for this workshop. We also wish to thank the associate director of the Center for Education, Patricia Morison, for her assistance with this work. We thank Susan Hunt for her editorial assistance on this report. Special thanks go to Andrew Tompkins for his management of the operational aspects of the committee meetings and production of this report. We also appreciate Lisa Alston's guidance on pertinent administrative issues throughout the project. The committee is particularly grateful to Kaeli Knowles, study director, for her tireless efforts throughout the project, from the time we assembled the steering committee and coordinated its work, to putting together a stimulating workshop, to preparing the manuscript for this report.

This report has been reviewed in draft form by individuals chosen for their diverse perspectives and technical expertise, in accordance with procedures approved by the Report Review Committee of the National Research Council. The purpose of this independent review is to provide candid and critical comments that will assist the institution in making the published report as sound as possible and to ensure that the report meets institutional standards for objectivity, evidence, and responsiveness to the study charge. The review comments and draft manuscript remain confidential to protect the integrity of the deliberative process.

We thank the following individuals for their participation in the review of this report: Eugene Johnson, American Institutes for Research, Washington, DC; Dorry Kenyon, Center for Applied Linguistics, Washington, DC; Kristen M. Kulongoski, Oregon Department of Community Colleges and Workforce Development; Lennox L. McLendon, National Adult Education Professional Development Consortium, Inc., Washington, DC; and Steve Reder, Department of Applied Linguistics, Portland State University.

Although the reviewers listed above have provided many constructive comments and suggestions, they were not asked to endorse the final draft of the report before its release. The review of this report was overseen by Milton Goldberg, National Alliance of Business, Washington, DC. Appointed by the National Research Council, he was responsible for making certain that an independent examination of this report was carried out in accordance with institutional procedures and that all review comments were carefully considered. Responsibility for the final content of this report rests entirely with the authoring committee and the institution.

Robert J. Mislevy
Chair

Contents

1

Introduction

The Workforce Investment Act (WIA), enacted by Congress in 1998, requires states to establish a comprehensive accountability system for adult education programs. The WIA mandates that states must gather data on several core measures, including the educational gain of adult learners. States and local programs have typically utilized standardized tests to monitor the progress of adult learners. Yet many states and local programs are also interested in more authentic approaches, such as using performance assessments to measure students' educational gain.

At the request of the U.S. Department of Education (DOEd) and the National Institute for Literacy, the National Research Council (NRC) established the Committee for the Workshop on Alternatives for Assessing Adult Education and Literacy Programs to consider the measurement issues of using performance assessment for accountability purposes. During the course of the study, the committee operated under the following charge:

> The Board on Testing and Assessment (BOTA) of the National Academies proposes to convene a workshop on developing alternative assessments for measuring and reporting learning gains in adult basic education and literacy programs. At the workshop, the characteristics of psychometrically strong performance assessments as outlined in the *Standards for Educational and Psychological Testing* (1999) will be examined. Factors that affect the usefulness of performance assessments will be analyzed, and issues associated with identifying and managing these factors will be explored. The information gathered, discussed, and summarized at this workshop will aid states in their data collection for the National Reporting System (NRS) that assesses the

impact of adult education instruction, and in their development of performance-based accountability systems.

To respond to this charge, the committee convened a workshop on December 12 and 13, 2001. The report that follows is a summary of the workshop. (The agenda for the workshop appears in Appendix A.)

WORKSHOP ON PERFORMANCE ASSESSMENTS FOR ADULT EDUCATION

In the United States, the nomenclature of adult education includes adult literacy, adult secondary education, and English for speakers of other languages (ESOL) services provided to undereducated and limited English proficient adults. Those receiving adult education services have diverse reasons for seeking additional education. With the passage of the WIA, the assessment of adult education students became mandatory—regardless of their reasons for seeking services. The law does allow the states and local programs flexibility in selecting the most appropriate assessment for the student. The purpose of the NRC's workshop was to explore issues related to efforts to measure learning gains in adult basic education programs, with a focus on performance-based assessments.

The two-day workshop consisted of seven panels and utilized two kinds of formats. In one format, the panel included presentations to the committee and workshop sponsors on relevant information related to a particular topic; there were five of these panels. At the end of each day, there was also a panel of discussants who were selected for their expertise in either measurement or adult education; these participants were asked to respond to the workshop presentations. The commentary and feedback of the discussants are found throughout the report.

The opening panel was designed to provide a broad policy context for the two days of discussions. An overview of assessment in the context of adult education and literacy systems was presented by John Comings, senior research associate lecturer on education and director of the National Center for the Study of Adult Learning and Literacy at Harvard Graduate School of Education. Mike Dean, at DOEd's Office of Vocational and Adult Education, presented an overview of the WIA and the NRS. Last, Sondra Stein, senior research associate at the National Institute for Literacy and the national director of Equipped for the Future (EFF), discussed EFF, a standards-based approach to defining and measuring results in the adult education and literacy system. The EFF standards for adult literacy and lifelong learning are presented later in the report. Please see Chapter 6 and Figure 6-1 for more information about EFF.

The topic of the second panel was developing performance assessments. This panel included Pamela Moss, associate professor in the School of Education at the University of Michigan, and Stephen Dunbar, professor of educational measurement and statistics at the University of Iowa. Moss was a member of the joint committee that, in 1999, revised the *Standards for Educational and Psychological Testing* of the American Educational Research Association (AERA), the American Psychological Association (APA), and the National Council on Measurement in Education (NCME). She presented a brief overview of the purpose and development process for the standards, highlighted the structure and organization of the standards, and discussed how they should be used in developing assessments. She also provided an example of the use of the standards to guide validity research on a K-12 test. Dunbar's presentation identified important psychometric factors to consider in developing performance assessment tasks. These factors included administration, scoring, and security issues as well as technical issues, such as maintaining reliability and developing comparable tasks.

The topic of the third panel was lessons learned from other contexts. The speakers, who represented a wide variety of disciplines and settings, shared their experiences in developing and implementing performance assessments in their fields. Their comments covered staff training, quality control, provisions for technical assistance, and cost considerations. This panel included Judy Alamprese, principal associate at Abt Associates; Eduardo Cascallar, principal research scientist at the American Institutes for Research; Myrna Manly, specialist in numeracy assessment at El Camino College (retired); Leah Bricker, senior program associate with Project 2061 at the American Association for the Advancement of Science; and Marcia Invernizzi and Joanne Meier, professors at the Curry School of Education at the University of Virginia.

A subgroup of this third panel focused on lessons learned from K-12 state assessments. Several states have implemented performance-based assessment systems at the K-12 level for accountability purposes. Representatives from two states presented their states' accountability models. Although neither model is directly aligned with the requirements of the WIA, the committee believed hearing about these experiences at the K-12 level would be a fruitful exercise. Mark Moody, assistant superintendent for planning, results, and information management at the Maryland Department of Education, discussed the Maryland School Performance Assessment Program (MSPAP). The model for MSPAP focuses on using performance-based assessments to hold schools accountable. Students' scores are reported only at the school level—no student-level scores are reported. Another kind of performance assessment used at the K-12 level consists of constructed-response questions in which students respond to a written prompt or short-answer questions. Kit Viator, administrator for student testing at the Massachusetts Department of Education, discussed the Massachusetts Comprehensive Assessment System (MCAS), which includes both selected-response and constructed-response questions.

The panel of discussants for the first day responded to measurement issues related to developing performance assessments. Panel members, all experts in adult education or assessment, were Cheryl Keenan, director of adult education at the Pennsylvania Department of Education; Jim Impara, director of the Buros Institute of Assessment Consultation and Outreach; and Richard Hill, founder and executive director of the National Center for the Improvement of Educational Assessment.

The fifth panel brought together several measurement experts to provide guidance on applying the *Standards* to the development and implementation of performance assessments in adult education. The panel members offered suggestions on possible approaches or models for performance assessments, discussed comparability issues inherent in the NRS, and outlined the steps for developing performance assessments. This panel included Mark Reckase, professor of measurement and quantitative methods at Michigan State University; Henry Braun, distinguished presidential appointee and managing director of literacy services at the Educational Testing Service (ETS); and Mari Pearlman, vice president of the Division of Teaching and Learning at ETS.

In the sixth panel, the implications of using performance assessments with the NRS were considered from a variety of perspectives including those of state directors, local program directors, and test publishers. In the final presentation in this panel, a state director considered the level of readiness of adult education systems for high-stakes assessment. The panel members were Fran Tracy-Mumford, director of adult education for the state of Delaware; Donna Miller-Parker, director at the Shoreline Community College in Seattle, Washington; Wendy Yen, vice president of research at K-12 Works, ETS; and Bob Bickerton, director of adult education for Massachusetts.

The final panel of discussants synthesized and responded to the measurement issues raised over both days of the workshop. This panel was composed of well-known statisticians with extensive knowledge about assessment: Ronald Hambleton, distinguished professor at the University of Massachusetts at Amherst; David Thissen, professor of psychology at the University of North Carolina at Chapel Hill; Barbara Plake, W.C. Meierhenry distinguished professor of educational psychology at the University of Nebraska, Lincoln, and director of the Oscar and Luella Buros Center for Testing and the Buros Institute of Mental Measurements; and Stephen Sireci, associate professor in research and evaluation methods at the University of Massachusetts at Amherst.

The workshop was structured to permit considerable discussion by presenters and participants. Following each speaker's presentation, substantial time was devoted to open discussion. In preparation for the workshop, speakers were given sets of questions to address during their presentations, and they were asked to supply written copies of their presentations in advance. Members of the workshop steering committee served as moderators for each panel.

After the workshop, the steering committee decided to commission several papers that either expanded or complemented presentations heard at the workshop and that would be useful for the sponsors and adult educators. The first paper is a practitioner's guide to developing performance assessment by Mari Pearlman of ETS. The paper will expand on her workshop presentation, "Performance Assessments for Adult Education: How to Design Performance Tasks." Lawrence Frase of George Mason University is also writing a paper on how advances in technology could address some of the assessment challenges facing the adult education community. Frase's paper will discuss how technology can facilitate computer-based testing such as adaptive and multi-level testing, new item formats and automated scoring procedures, and professional development and training of teachers. Finally, the committee and sponsors were interested in learning how performance assessments in adult education systems were implemented internationally. The third paper will include a discussion on how countries have developed and utilized alternative assessments. Committee members thought that information on the operations of international systems with performance-based assessments of numeracy, literacy, and/or language (English Language Learning/ESOL/ESL) would be useful to the sponsor. These papers can be obtained by contacting DOEd's Office of Vocational and Adult Education or the National Institute for Literacy.

ORGANIZATION OF THE REPORT

The purpose of this report is to capture the discussions and major points made during the workshop in order to assist states and local adult education programs in their development and implementation of performance assessments. Many speakers alluded to a number of measurement concepts throughout the workshop. To assist readers not fully acquainted with measurement issues who may desire additional information about various topics, there are referrals to measurement texts and relevant journal articles throughout the report. It is important to note that as a workshop summary, this report is intended only to highlight the key issues identified by stakeholders and participants who attended the workshop; it does not attempt to establish consensus on findings and recommendations.

As described above, the WIA of 1998 mandated that states develop an accountability system for adult education programs and report results on an annual basis. The DOEd established the NRS (National Reporting System) for states to use to gather and report data from their local programs. With the passage of the WIA, the stakes have risen for state and local adult education programs. The field of adult education is in a period of transition as states establish accountability systems that adhere to the federal requirements of the WIA. Chapter 2 of this report summarizes the specific measurement and reporting requirements of the WIA and the NRS and delineates the local and state responsibilities for implementing the NRS. The chapter also provides an overview of the population, structure, and resources of states and local programs to respond to these mandates. Chapter 3 discusses the purposes of assessment and test design.

Chapter 4 examines the AERA/APA/NCME *Standards* as they relate to developing and implementing a performance assessment. Psychometric factors such as reliability, validity, generalizability, and fairness must be considered in developing quality assessments. Chapter 5 addresses the process of developing performance assessments for the NRS. Chapter 6 highlights the challenges and constraints associated with implementing the NRS, with a particular focus on performance assessments. Finally, Chapter 7 explores some options and strategies that could be useful for states and local programs in resolving the issues associated with implementing performance assessments to provide data required by the NRS.

2

Background

Accountability is a fact of life in the current educational setting, not only in the United States but in many other countries. Educational programs that are funded by public monies are increasingly being asked to account not only for how they expend public resources, but for the extent to which these expenditures result in educational outcomes that are valued by stakeholders. Standardized assessments are believed by some to be one of the most powerful levers that policy makers have for influencing what occurs in the classroom in a high-stakes accountability system. A premise of high-stakes accountability is that instruction and student learning will be improved by holding teachers and/or students accountable for test results. Many have argued that there can be negative consequences associated with high-stakes assessment as well. These include teaching to the test, narrowing of the curriculum, cheating, and making improper or inaccurate high-stakes decisions based on one test result (National Research Council [NRC], 1999b).

There are a number of challenges associated with using tests accurately and fairly for accountability purposes. Sometimes, performance assessments, which generally require test takers to demonstrate their skills and knowledge in a manner that closely resembles a real-life situation or setting, are seen as solutions to the limitations of other assessments such as multiple-choice tests (NRC, 2001a). In this report, the use of performance assessments in adult education for high-stakes purposes is discussed. In order to describe the workshop discussions about benefits and issues associated with performance assessments in several areas of the report background information is provided on pertinent measurement concepts. Many of the challenges identified in this report may be relevant to other kinds of tests and the broader accountability system of adult education.

WORKFORCE INVESTMENT ACT AND THE NATIONAL REPORTING SYSTEM

The passage of the Workforce Investment Act (WIA) of 1998, Title II (Public Law 105-220), mandated an accountability system for state adult education systems. Under the WIA, the U.S. Department of Education (DOEd) was required to negotiate levels of performance with each state for "core measures of performance" related to

> (i) Demonstrated improvements in literacy skill levels in reading, writing, and speaking the English language, numeracy, problem solving, English language acquisition, and other literacy skills.
>
> (ii) Placement in, retention in, or completion of, postsecondary education, training, unsubsidized employment or career advancement.
>
> (iii) Receipt of a secondary school diploma or its recognized equivalent (Public Law 105, Section 212).

The DOEd developed the National Reporting System (NRS) in order to support the development of the comprehensive accountability system required by the WIA. Within the NRS, students are administered an assessment at entry to an adult education program and then take a posttest after a period of instruction determined by each state. States are given the flexibility to select the assessment of their choice to measure students' progress on an annual basis. The assessments may be standardized tests or performance-based assessments that reflect the skill areas identified in the NRS educational functioning levels.

The NRS specifies six educational functioning levels for both adult basic education (ABE) and English as a second language (ESL). These functioning levels include brief descriptions of the skills students are expected to demonstrate at each of six levels in specific subject areas. The subject areas for ABE are reading and writing, numeracy, and functional and workplace skills. For ESL, the subject areas are speaking and listening, reading and writing, and functional and workplace skills. The functioning levels are displayed in Table 2-1 and described in more detail later in this chapter. The states report the percentage of students who move from one functioning level to the next.

In his presentation, Mike Dean, of the DOEd's Office of Vocational and Adult Education, explained that the NRS provides the methodologies and structure for the collection, analysis, and reporting of data on the core measures from the local level to the state level to the federal government. Dean stressed the importance of producing valid and reliable results and emphasized the fact that the whole system depends on the comparability of data across states, that is, similar scores reported for performance on Program A and Program C should reflect students' mastery of similar skills and knowledge. Dean acknowledged the complexity of achieving comparability when different assessments are being used in different programs and different states.

The WIA also includes incentives for states that exceed the levels of performance agreed to by the DOEd. The agreement on the performance levels takes into account statutory criteria.[1] The criteria include factors such as the characteristics of participants at entry to the program, the services or instruction that are provided within a program, and the extent to which the performance levels promote continuous improvement in student performance. The performance levels were approved for the first three years of the five-year state plan period (7/1/99–6/30/02) with the performance levels for years four and five (7/1/02–6/30/04) being approved in 2002.

Yet in order for state adult education programs to be eligible for the incentives, other federally supported programs are simultaneously required to show improvement and meet particular goals. These other programs include Title I (employment services and job training) administered by the Department of Labor and, under a separate act, the Carl D. Perkins Vocational–Technical Education Act Amendments of 1998 (Public Law 105–332). All three federally supported programs, WIA Titles I and II and Perkins, must exceed their negotiated levels of performance in order to qualify for an incentive grant award that can range from $750,000 to $3 million. For states that qualify for incentive grants, the governor has latitude in making allocations of the grant among the three major programs. In addition, the DOEd is required to provide an annual report to Congress

[1]The law can be located at http://thomas.loc.gov/cgi-bin/bdquery/z?d105:HR01385:|TOM:/bss/d105query.html. [April 24, 2002].

TABLE 2-1 Educational Functioning Level Descriptors—Adult Basic Education Levels

Literacy Level	Basic Reading and Writing
Beginning ABE Literacy Benchmarks: TABE (5-6) scale scores (grade level 0-1.9): Total Reading: 529 and below Total Math: 540 and below Total Language: 599 and below TABE (7-8) scale scores (grade level 0-1.9): Reading: 367 and below Total Math: 313 and below Language: 391 and below CASAS: 200 and below AMES (B, ABE) scale scores (grade level 0-1.9): Reading: 500 and below Total Math: 476 and below Communication: 496 and below ABLE scale scores (grade level 0-1.9): Reading: 523 and below Math: 521 and below	• Individual has no or minimal reading and writing skills. • May have little or no comprehension of how print corresponds to spoken language and may have difficulty using a writing instrument. • At upper range of this level, individual can recognize, read and write letters and numbers, but has a limited understanding of connected prose and may need frequent re-reading. • Can write a number of basic sight words and familiar words and phrases. • May also be able to write simple sentences or phrase, including simple messages. • Can write basic personal information. • Narrative writing is disorganized and unclear, inconsistently uses simple punctuation (e.g., periods, commas, question marks). • Contains frequent spelling errors.
Beginning Basic Education Benchmarks: TABE (5-6) scale scores (grade level 2-3.9): Total Reading: 530-679 Total Math: 541–677 Total Language: 600–977 TABE (7-8) scale scores (grade level 2-3.9): Reading: 368–460 Total Math: 314–441 Language: 392-490 CASAS: 201-210 AMES (B, ABE) scale scores (grade level 2-3.9): Reading: 503–510 Total Math: 477–492 Communication: 498–506 ABLE scale scores (grade level 2-3.9): Reading: 525–612 Math: 530–591	• Individual can read simple material on familiar subjects and comprehend simple compound sentences in single or linked paragraphs containing a familiar vocabulary. • Can write simple notes and messages on familiar situations, but lacks clarity and focus. • Sentence structure lacks variety, but shows some control of basic grammar (e.g., present and past tense), and consistent use of punctuation (e.g., periods, capitalization).

Numeracy Skills	Functional and Workplace Skills
• Individual has little or no recognition of numbers or simple counting skills or may have only minimal skills, such as the ability to add or subtract single digit numbers.	• Individual has little or no ability to read basic signs or maps, can provide limited personal information on simple forms. • The individual can handle routine entry-level jobs that require little or no basic written communication or computational skills and no knowledge of computers or other technology.
• Individual can count, add and subtract three digit numbers; can perform multiplication through 12. • Can identify simple fractions and perform other simple arithmetic operations.	• Individual is able to read simple directions, signs, and maps; fill out simple forms requiring basic personal information; write phone messages and make simple change. • There is minimal knowledge of, and experience with, using computers and related technology. • The individual can handle basic entry-level jobs that require minimal literacy skills. • Can recognize very short, explicit, pictorial texts, e.g., understands logos related to worker safety before using a piece of machinery. • Can read want ads and complete job applications.

Table continued on next page

TABLE 2-1 Continued

Literacy Level	Basic Reading and Writing
Low Intermediate Basic Education Benchmarks: TABE (5-6) scale scores (grade level 6-8.9): Total Reading: 723–761 Total Math: 730–776 Total Language: 706–730 TABE (7-8) scale scores (grade level 6-8.9): Reading: 518–566 Total Math: 506–565 Language: 524–559 CASAS: 221–235 AMES (C and D, ABE) scale scores (grade level 6-8.9): Reading (C): 525–612 Reading (D): 522–543 Total Math (C): 510–627 Total Math (D): 509–532 Communication (C): 516–611 Communication (D): 516–523 ABLE scale scores (grade level 6-8.9): Reading: 646–680 Math: 643–693	• Individual can read text on familiar subjects that have a simple and clear underlying structure (e.g., clear main idea, chronological order). • Can use context to determine meaning. • Can interpret actions required in specific written directions. • Can write simple paragraphs with main idea and supporting detail on familiar topics (e.g., daily activities, personal issues) by recombining learned vocabulary and structures. • Can self and peer edit for spelling and punctuation errors.

Numeracy Skills	Functional and Workplace Skills
• Individual can perform with high accuracy all four basic math operations using whole numbers up to three digits. • Can identify and use all basic mathematical symbols.	• Individual is able to handle basic reading, writing, and computational tasks related to life roles, such as completing medical forms, order forms, or job applications. • Can read simple charts, graphs, labels, and payroll stubs and simple authentic material if familiar with the topic. • The individual can use simple computer programs and perform a sequence of routine tasks given direction using technology (e.g., fax machine, computer operation). • The individual can qualify for entry-level jobs that require following basic written instructions and diagrams with assistance, such as oral clarification. • Can write a short report or message to fellow workers. • Can read simple dials and scales and take routine measurements.

Table continued on next page

TABLE 2-1 Continued

Literacy Level	Basic Reading and Writing
High Intermediate Basic Education Benchmarks: TABE (5-6) scale scores (grade level 6-8.9): Total Reading: 723–761 Total Math: 730–776 Total Language: 706–730 TABE (7-8) scale scores (grade level 6-8.9): Reading: 518– 66 Total Math: 506–565 Language: 524–559 CASAS: 221–235 AMES (C and D, ABE) scale scores (grade level 6-8.9): Reading (C): 525–612 Reading (D): 522–543 Total Math (C): 510–627 Total Math (D): 509–532 Communication (C): 516–611 Communication (D): 516–523 ABLE scale scores (grade level 6-8.9): Reading: 646–680 Math: 643–693	• Individual is able to read simple descriptions and narratives on familiar subjects or from which new vocabulary can be determined by context. • Can make some minimal inferences about familiar texts and compare and contrast information from such texts, but not consistently. • The individual can write simple narrative descriptions and short essays on familiar topics. • Has consistent use of basic punctuation, but makes grammatical errors with complex structures.

Numeracy Skills	Functional and Workplace Skills
• Individual can perform all four basic math operations with whole numbers and fractions. • Can determine correct math operations for solving narrative math problems and can convert fractions to decimals and decimals to factions. • Can perform basic operations on fractions.	• Individual is able to handle basic life skills tasks such as graphs, charts, and labels, and can follow multi-step diagrams. • Can read authentic materials on familiar topics, such as simple employee handbooks and payroll stubs. • Can complete forms such as a job application and reconcile a bank statement. • Can handle jobs that involve following simple written instructions and diagrams. • Can read procedural texts, where the information is supported by diagrams, to remedy a problem, such as locating a problem with a machine or carrying out repairs using a repair manual. • The individual can learn or work with most basic computer software, such as using a word processor to produce own texts. • Can follow simple instructions for using technology.

Table continued on next page

TABLE 2-1 Continued

Literacy Level	Basic Reading and Writing
Low Adult Secondary Education Benchmarks: TABE (5-6) scale scores (grade level 9–10.9): Total Reading: 762–775 Total Math: 777–789 Total Language: 731–743 TABE (7-8) scale scores (grade level 9–10.9): Reading: 567–595 Total Math: 566–594 Language: 560–585 CASAS: 236–245 AMES (E, ABE) scale scores (grade level 9-10.9): Reading: 544–561 Total Math: 534–548 Communication: 527–535 ABLE scale scores (grade level 9-10.9): Reading: 682–697 Math: 643–716	• Individual can comprehend expository writing and identify spelling, punctuation, and grammatical errors. • Can comprehend a variety of materials such as periodicals and non-technical journals on common topics. • Can comprehend library reference materials and compose multi-paragraph essays. • Can listen to oral instructions and write an accurate synthesis of them. • Can identify the main idea in reading selections and use a variety of context issues to determine meaning. • Writing is organized and cohesive with few mechanical errors. • Can write using a complex sentence structure. • Can write personal notes and letters that accurately reflect thoughts.

Numeracy Skills	Functional and Workplace Skills
• Individual can perform all basic math functions with whole numbers, decimals and fractions. • Can interpret and solve simple algebraic equations, tables and graphs, and can develop own tables and graphs. • Can use math in business transactions.	• Individual is able or can learn to follow simple multi-step directions and read common legal forms and manuals. • Can integrate information from texts, charts, and graphs. • Can create and use tables and graphs. • Can complete forms and applications and complete resumes. • Can perform jobs than require interpreting information from various sources and writing or explaining tasks to other workers. • Is proficient using computers and can use most common computer applications. • Can understand the impact of using different technologies. • Can interpret the appropriate use of new software and technology.

Table continued on next page

TABLE 2-1 Continued

Literacy Level	Basic Reading and Writing
High Adult Secondary Education Benchmarks: TABE (5-6) scale scores (grade level 11-12): Total Reading: 776 and above Total Math: 790 and above Total Language: 744 and above TABE (7-8) scale scores (grade level 11-12): Reading: 596 and above Total Math: 595 and above Language: 586 and above CASAS: 246 and above AMES (E, ABE) scale score (grade level 11-12): Reading: 565 and above Total Math: 551 and above Communication: 538 and above ABLE scale scores (grade level 11-12): Reading: 699 and above Math: 717 and above	• Individual can comprehend, explain, and analyze information from a variety of literacy works, including primary source materials and professional journals. • Can use context cues and higher order processes to interpret meaning of written material. • Writing is cohesive with clearly expressed ideas supported by relevant detail. • Can use varied and complex sentence structures with few mechanical errors.

Numeracy Skills	Functional and Workplace Skills
• Individual can make mathematical estimates of time and space and can apply principles of geometry to measure angles, lines and surfaces. • Can also apply trigonometric functions.	• Individuals are able to read technical information and complex manuals. • Can comprehend some college level books and apprenticeship manuals. • Can function in most job situations involving higher order thinking. • Can read text and explain a procedure about a complex and unfamiliar work procedure, such as operating a complex piece of machinery. • Can evaluate new work situations and processes, can work productively and collaboratively in groups and serve as facilitator and reporter of group work. • The individual is able to use common software and learn new software applications. • Can define the purpose of new technology and software and select appropriate technology. • Can adapt use of software or technology to new situations and can instruct others, in written or oral form, on software and technology use.

Table continued on next page

TABLE 2-1 Continued

Literacy Level	Speaking and Listening
Beginning ESL Literacy Benchmarks: CASAS (Life Skills): 180 and below SPL (Speaking): 01 SPL (Reading and Writing): 01 Oral BEST: 015 Literacy BEST: 07	• Individual cannot speak or understand English, or understands only isolated words or phrases.
Beginning ESL Benchmarks: CASAS (Life Skills): 181–200 SPL (Speaking): 2–3 SPL (Reading and Writing): 2 Oral BEST: 16–41 Literacy BEST: 8–46	• Individual can understand frequently used words in context and very simple phrases spoken slowly with some repetition. • There is little communicative output and only in the most routine situations. • Little or no control over basic grammar. • Survival needs can be communicated simply, and there is some understanding of simple questions.

Basic Reading and Writing	Functional and Workplace Skills
• Individual has no or minimal reading or writing skills in any language. • May have little or no comprehension of how print corresponds to spoken language and may have difficulty using a writing instrument.	• Individual functions minimally or not at all in English and can communicate only through gestures or a few isolated words, such as name and other personal information. • May recognize only common signs or symbols (e.g., stop sign, product logos). • Can handle only very routine entry-level jobs that do not require oral or written communication in English. • There is no knowledge or use of computers or technology.
• Individual can recognize, read, and write numbers and letters, but has a limited understanding of connected prose and may need frequent re-reading. • Can write a limited number of basic sight words and familiar words and phrases. • May also be able to write simple sentences or phrases, including very simple messages. • Can write basic personal information. • Narrative writing is disorganized and unclear. • Inconsistently uses simple punctuation (e.g., periods, commas, question marks). • Contains frequent errors in spelling.	• Individual functions with difficulty in situations related to immediate needs and in limited social situations. • Has some simple oral communication abilities using simple learned and repeated phrases. • May need frequent repetition. • Can provide personal information on simple forms. • Can recognize common forms of print found in the home and environment, such as labels and product names. • Can handle routine entry-level jobs that require only the most basic written or oral English communication and in which job tasks can be demonstrated. • There is minimal knowledge or experience using computers or technology.

Table continued on next page

TABLE 2-1 Continued

Literacy Level	Speaking and Listening
Low Intermediate ESL Benchmarks: CASAS (Life Skills): 201–210 SPL (Speaking): 4 SPL (Reading and Writing): 5 Oral BEST: 42–50 Literacy BEST: 47–53	• Individual can understand simple learned phrases and limited new phrases containing familiar vocabulary spoken slowly with frequent repetition. • Can ask and respond to questions using such phrases. • Can express basic survival needs and participate in some routine social conversations, although with some difficulty. • Has some control of basic grammar.
High Intermediate ESL Benchmarks: CASAS (Life Skills): 211–220 SPL (Speaking): 5 SPL (Reading and Writing): 6 Oral BEST: 51–57 Literacy BEST: 54–65	• Individual can understand learned phrases and short new phrases containing familiar vocabulary spoken slowly, with some repetition. • Can communicate basic survival needs with some help. • Can participate in conversation in limited social situations and use new phrases with hesitation. • Relies on description and concrete terms. • There is inconsistent control of more complex grammar.

Basic Reading and Writing	Functional and Workplace Skills
• Individual can read simple material on familiar subjects and comprehend simple and compound sentences in single or linked paragraphs containing a familiar vocabulary. • Can write simple notes and messages on familiar situations, but lacks clarity and focus. • Sentence structure lacks variety, but shows some control of basic grammar (e.g., past and present tense) and consistent use of punctuation (e.g., periods and capitalization).	• Individual can interpret simple directions and schedules, signs and maps. • Can fill out simple forms, but needs support on some documents that are not simplified. • Can handle routine entry-level jobs that involve some written or oral English communication, but in which job tasks can be demonstrated. • Individual can use simple computer programs and can perform a sequence of routine tasks given directions using technology (e.g., fax machine, computer).
• Individual can read text on familiar subjects that have a simple and clear underlying structure (e.g., clear main idea, chronological order). • Can use context to determine meaning. • Can interpret actions required in specific written directions. • Can write simple paragraphs with main idea and supporting detail on familiar topics (e.g., daily activities, personal issues) by recombining learned vocabulary and structures. • Can self and peer edit for spelling and punctuation errors.	• Individual can meet basic survival and social needs. • Can follow simple oral and written instruction and has some ability to communicate on the telephone on familiar subjects. • Can write messages and notes related to basic needs; complete basic medical forms and job applications. • Can handle jobs that involve basic oral instructions and written communication in tasks that can be clarified orally. • The individual can work with or learn basic computer software, such as word processing. • Can follow simple instructions for using technology.

Table continued on next page

TABLE 2-1 Continued

Literacy Level	Speaking and Listening
Low Advanced ESL Benchmarks: CASAS (Life Skills): 221–235 SPL (Speaking): 6 SPL (Reading and Writing): 7 Oral BEST: 58–64 Literacy BEST: 65 and above	• Individual can converse on many everyday subjects and some subjects with unfamiliar vocabulary, but may need repetition, rewording, or slower speech. • Can speak creatively, but with hesitation. • Can clarify general meaning by rewording and has control of basic grammar. • Understands descriptive and spoken narrative and can comprehend abstract concepts in familiar contexts.
High Advanced ESL Benchmarks: CASAS (Life Skills): 236–245 SPL (Speaking): 7 SPL (Reading and Writing): 8 Oral BEST: 65 and above	• Individual can understand and participate effectively in face-to-face conversations on everyday subjects spoken at normal speed. • Can converse and understand independently in survival, work, and social situations. • Can expand on basic ideas in conversation, but with some hesitation. • Can clarify general meaning and control basic grammar, although still lacks total control over complex structures.

SOURCE: National Reporting System (2002).

<table>
<tr><th>Basic Reading and Writing</th><th>Functional and Workplace Skills</th></tr>
<tr><td>• Individual is able to read simple descriptions and narratives on familiar subjects or from which new vocabulary can be determined by context.
• Can make some minimal inferences about familiar texts and compare and contrast information from such texts, but not consistently.
• The individual can write simple narrative descriptions and short essays on familiar topics, such as customs in native country.
• Has consistent use of basic punctuation, but makes grammatical errors with complex structures.</td><td>• Individual can function independently to meet most survival needs and can communicate on the telephone on familiar topics.
• Can interpret simple charts and graphics.
• Can handle jobs that require simple oral and written instructions, multi-step diagrams, and limited public interaction.
• The individual can use all basic software applications, understand the impact of technology, and select the correct technology in a new situation.</td></tr>
<tr><td>• Individual can read authentic materials on everyday subjects and can handle most reading related to life roles.
• Can consistently and fully interpret descriptive narratives on familiar topics and gain meaning from unfamiliar topics.
• Uses increased control of language and meaning-making strategies to gain meaning of unfamiliar texts.
• The individual can write multi-paragraph essays with a clear introduction and development of ideas.
• Writing contains well-formed sentences, appropriate mechanics and spelling, and few grammatical errors.</td><td>• Individual has a general ability to use English effectively to meet most routine social and work situations.
• Can interpret routine charts, graphs and tables and complete forms.
• Has high ability to communicate on the telephone and understand radio and television.
• Can meet work demands that require reading and writing and can interact with the public.
• The individual can use common software and learn new applications.
• Can define the purpose of software and select new applications.
• Can instruct others in use of software and technology.</td></tr>
</table>

that details and compares the performance of each state with respect to the core measures of performance. These public reports are shared with state governors and the chief executive officers of the agency in each state that has jurisdiction over the WIA Title II program. Finally, the state agency responsible for administering WIA Title II must consider the performance, with respect to the core measures, of local programs when it makes funding decisions about these programs.

These provisions for incentive grants and high-profile state performance reports establish high stakes for the ABE performance accountability system. First of all, $750,000 to $3 million for incentive grant awards is more than some states receive under their entire annual allocation under WIA Title II. Second, the tripartite structure for qualifying for these grants ensures that governors will be well aware of which local ABE programs may have failed to qualify their state for such an award. Third, the public reports that must be provided to Congress and other elected and policy leaders, which compare the performance of states on these measures, will be used to assess the appropriateness of federal and related state expenditures on this program. Fourth, depending on their level of performance, local programs may lose all or part of their funding and, because many are heavily dependent on this funding, their ability to provide ABE services will be at risk.

MEASUREMENT AND REPORTING REQUIREMENTS OF THE NATIONAL REPORTING SYSTEM

The WIA required the establishment of a comprehensive accountability system and the annual measurement and reporting of data on students' performance in reading, writing, and numeracy. The NRS established the specific reporting requirements for state and local adult education programs and included a measure of educational gain in the content areas. Under the NRS guidelines, students are assessed in the skill areas most relevant to their needs or to program curriculum during intake. If students are assessed in multiple content areas and have different abilities across those content areas, the local program should place the student according to his or her lowest functioning level. The local programs then make decisions about appropriate instruction. All students must also be assessed at least one more time during the program year.

The NRS Educational Functioning Levels

The students' scores at intake (pretest) and on the follow-up (posttest) assessments are examined in light of the NRS educational levels. There are six educational functioning levels for both adult basic education (ABE) and English as a second language (ESL) (see Table 2-1). The six functioning levels for ABE are: (1) Beginning ABE Literacy; (2) Beginning Basic Education; (3) Low Intermediate Basic Education; (4) High Intermediate Basic Education; (5) Low Adult Secondary Education; and (6) High Adult Secondary Education. The six levels for ESL are: (1) Beginning ESL Literacy; (2) Beginning ESL; (3) Low Intermediate ESL; (4) High Intermediate ESL; (5) Low Advanced ESL; and (6) High Advanced ESL.

Each of the NRS educational functioning levels includes a brief narrative description of the skills required for a student to be placed at that particular level. For example, the Beginning ABE Literacy functioning level in reading and writing is described as follows:

- Individual has no or minimal reading and writing skills.
- May have little or no comprehension of how print corresponds to spoken language and may have difficulty using a writing instrument.
- At upper range of this level, individual can recognize, read and write letters and numbers, but has a limited understanding of connected prose and may need frequent re-reading.
- Can write a number of basic sight words and familiar words and phrases.
- May also be able to write simple sentences or phrases, including simple messages.
- Can write basic personal information.
- Narrative writing is disorganized and unclear, inconsistently uses simple punctuation (e.g., periods, commas, question marks).
- Contains frequent spelling errors.

In numeracy, the Beginning ABE Literacy level states:

- Individual has little or no recognition of numbers or simple counting skills or may have only minimal skills, such as the ability to add or subtract single digit numbers.

In functional and workplace skills, the Beginning ABE Literacy level states:

- Individual has little or no ability to read basic signs or maps, can provide limited personal information on simple forms.
- The individual can handle routine entry-level jobs that require little or no basic written communication or computational skills and no knowledge of computers or other technology.

Benchmarks for Educational Functioning Levels

For several of the standardized tests commonly used in adult education, benchmark scale scores are provided for each educational level as examples of how students functioning at that level would perform on the tests. These benchmark scores were set by the test publisher at the request of the DOEd. Accordingly, the test publisher was instructed to determine the test score range for which examinees would be expected to possess the skills described for each functioning level.

The standardized tests with benchmarks on the NRS consist primarily of multiple-choice items. They are (1) the Comprehensive Adult Standard Assessment System (CASAS-Life Skills or Employability); (2) Test of Adult Basic Education (TABE); (3) the Adult Basic Learning Examination (ABLE); (4) the Adult Measure of Educational Skills (AMES); (5) Student Performance Levels (SPL) for ESL in both speaking and reading; and (6) oral scores of the Basic English Skills Test (BEST) for ESL. For example, for the CASAS, a score of 200 is considered to be the cutoff score for the Beginning ABE Literacy level. For TABE (Form 7-8), a score of 367 for reading is considered to be the cutoff score for this level. (Full descriptions of the functioning levels and benchmark scores for standardized tests appear in Table 2-1.)

The guidelines for the NRS acknowledge that "the tests should not be considered equivalent, however, and do not necessarily measure the same skills." The guidelines also state that the "tests are offered only as examples and their inclusion does not imply that these tests must or should be used in the determination of educational functioning levels" (DOEd, 2001a:40).

The educational functioning levels are used to measure educational gain. The difference between the students' functioning level at intake (or at pretest) and at the follow-up assessment (or posttest) is what determines educational gain. After an established period of instructional hours, if a student's skills have improved enough so that he or she can move to a higher educational functioning level, an "advance" is recorded for that student.

IMPLEMENTING THE NRS

Local Responsibilities

The NRS has been designed so that all local programs administer a standardized assessment using valid and uniform procedures and then enter data for each individual into the state data collection system. The programs must provide information on the three types of core measures (outcome, descriptive, and participatory) for each student as well as demographic information, attendance hours, individual student goals, and assessment results. Programs must also submit descriptive information on the roles and responsibilities of all staff members, budgetary information, and reporting timeline as determined by state policy.

According to the NRS guidelines (DOEd, 2001a), the information programs collect is either aggregated at the local level and used to produce reports on the overall program, or it is aggregated for reporting by the state. Whether the aggregation occurs at the local or state level, reports to the states typically indicate the number of students at each functioning level for ABE and ESL, the number recommended for advancement, the percentage of students advancing by level, and the average number of contact hours per student before advancement. The federal government anticipates that the data collected at the local level will be useful for program management and program improvement efforts.

State Responsibilities

States are responsible for determining the assessment policy and procedures that local programs must use to gather and report information about individuals participating in each program. This includes deciding the skill areas in which to assess students, choosing the standardized test and assessment procedure that local programs should use, and determining when to conduct the posttest. The posttest should be administered after a set instructional period, expressed either in hours (e.g., after 40 hours of instruction) or months (e.g., the last two weeks in May or the last week of instruction). For the purpose of NRS reporting, a different form of the same test should be used for the posttest. If states decide to use a performance assessment, the tasks used for the pretest and the posttest should measure the same content and skills. States are responsible for training and monitoring staff in the proper use, administration, and scoring of the chosen assessment, which is especially important with performance-based assessment.

The states are also responsible for developing a database system for the collection of individual student information. States could choose either to distribute software for collection of NRS information to each local program or to maintain a centrally located internet data collection system. States are required to evaluate each local program's performance on the outcome measures as one factor in determining local funding. One area of particular interest to the states is how well the local programs are addressing the needs of specific population groups, such as low-income students or adults in family literacy programs. To obtain this information, the software system must have the capability to report by individual program and by student population groups. Finally, states must also provide technical assistance to local program staff as needed and conduct periodic quality control reviews of local programs.

States must set performance standards on each core measure discussed earlier, and they are eligible for incentive awards if they meet these standards. For the core outcome measure that includes educational gain, the performance standards include the percentage of students who will meet or exceed each educational functioning level. The states are also required to meet expectations on the other outcome measures. The performance standards for each of these are negotiated between every state and the federal government.

States are responsible for reporting aggregated data to the federal government in order to be eligible for WIA funding. The report must include information on all the core measures, and reporting tables have been developed to facilitate reporting. Each state must submit seven reporting tables, including a table on educational gain and attendance by educational functioning level.

Federal Responsibilities

The DOEd has published the NRS, which identifies in broad terms the standards that state and local programs must meet. The data collected through the NRS will be used by the DOEd to demonstrate program effectiveness to Congress and to determine state incentive awards. Under WIA, the role of the DOEd also includes providing assistance to states in understanding and implementing the requirements of the NRS. The guidelines for the NRS were commissioned by the DOEd as part of the effort to develop more specific and precise requirements related to the use of performance assessments permitted under the NRS (DOEd, 2001a). It is clearly relevant to the DOEd's responsibilities to ensure that the quality of data is commensurate with their uses and collected in line with the practices of the *Standards for Educational and Psychological Testing* (American Educational Research Association [AERA] et al., 1999). It was noted at the workshop that the DOEd has assumed a quality assurance role with respect to the implementation by states of similar ESEA (Elementary and Secondary Education Act) Title I requirements; this model could be helpful to DOEd's Division of Adult Education and Literacy.

AN OVERVIEW OF THE U.S. ADULT BASIC EDUCATION PROGRAM

Appropriations for WIA Title II are authorized through federal fiscal year 2003, but because education funds are generally appropriated nine months in advance, fiscal year 2003 funds will be allocated to states for program year 2004 (July 2003 to June 2004). The Title II appropriation for program year 2002 is $565.1 million, with the major portion of this funding being a direct allocation to the states. States received between $750,000 and $52 million for 2001 (see Appendix C for a list of allocations for each state). State allocations are based on the number of non-high school graduates between 16 and 60 who are not currently enrolled in school according to census data.

For 2002, the DOEd has budgeted about $10 million for incentive grants to states that exceed the levels of performance they negotiated with the DOEd. As previously mentioned, if a state receives the incentive grants, the governor will make decisions about the allocation of funds among WIA Title I and II and Perkins programs. The DOEd also has $9.5 million for national programs this year. Over the last decade, the typical annual appropriation for national programs was about $6 million, which generally covered developmental initiatives, including activities related to the assessment challenges highlighted later in this report. Finally, the National Institute for Literacy receives $6.56 million, including a $1 million allocation for the Equipped for the Future initiative. In fiscal year 2002, an additional $8 million was provided to the National Center for Education Statistics to support the decennial National Assessment of Adult Literacy—a cost and an appropriation that will not recur until the next national assessment.

The major portion of federal adult basic education allocations to states (not less than 82.5 percent) must be used for grants to local providers of adult basic education services. In her presentation, Cheryl Keenan noted that under the law, state administration is capped at 5 percent, and state leadership funding from the federal government is capped at 12.5 percent. To provide context, she reported that in Pennsylvania, which is a "rich cousin" to other states, the state leadership fund represents approximately $2 million. For 2001, states received between $94,000 and $6.5 million in leadership funds. This last category supports professional development, technical assistance, evaluation, and a range of other developmental initiatives, and includes investments to develop, improve, and maintain assessments used by the state. Keenan noted that Pennsylvania has chosen to focus the majority of its $2 million leadership funding on staff development and the implementation of the performance accountability system (using standardized commercial assessments) required by the WIA. Kennan pointed out that states would have to decide to prioritize development of performance assessments over other issues given the limited leadership funds available. Also, several states do not appropriate state funds to match any of the federal investment, and of those that do, few allow state funding to be used for developmental purposes.

A wide range of public and private nonprofit entities are eligible for WIA Title II-funded grants, which are competitively awarded by states to provide adult basic education services. School districts, colleges, community-based organizations (and other nonprofits), correctional facilities, libraries, and other municipal agencies are recipients of these grants. Most states award grants almost exclusively to school districts, several almost exclusively to community colleges, and a small number of states award grants to a diverse mix of eligible entities. Grants to local programs cover an extraordinarily wide range, from under $1,000 to well over $1 million. A small number of states provide a few million dollars to each of their largest programs.

The number of program staff can range from one part-time coordinator to more than 100 professionals. In his presentation, John Comings noted that nationally for 1998, 13 percent of staff were full-time, 39 percent were part-time, and 48 percent were volunteers (see www.ed.gov/offices/OVAE/.html. [April 29, 2002]). Turnover among paid staff averages 30 percent per year. Administrative support can be quite limited. For instance, Donna Miller-Parker commented that her midsize program enrolls 1,000 students per year but has only one full-time coordinator (who is also responsible for other programs), one clerical staff person, and one student adviser. She noted that her college's situation is considered "pretty good" for an ABE program in her state.

In many states, professional development has been handled through the funding of a state literacy resource center, which may be part of a regional consortium. In his presentation, Bob Bickerton, director of adult education for Massachusetts, said that, with a few notable exceptions, per capita funding for teacher training is limited. For example, the teachers in Miller-Parker's program are only paid for their contact time with students; this makes it difficult to engage them in professional development and other program development and support activities. If she wants to plan a professional development activity for her teachers, Miller-Parker either cancels a class or offers some kind of incentive for teachers to participate on their own time. Keenan added that in Pennsylvania, as in many other states, there are no specific requirements for certification as an adult education teacher. Hence, Pennsylvania uses the bulk of its state leadership funds on training teachers, because it cannot assume that teachers are entering the field with the preservice type of knowledge those in other areas of education have. Other funds are devoted to implementing accountability systems required by WIA, including building and maintaining sophisticated data systems and providing tech support to the local programs that use them. Keenan concluded that the vast majority of states do not have great resources to invest in test development.

In program year 2000, approximately 2.9 million adults participated in WIA Title II-funded programs. In general, to be eligible for ABE services a person must be above the age of compulsory school attendance (as determined by each state) and (a) lack the level of skills expected of a high school graduate (most states enroll both high school noncompleters and undereducated high school graduates); and/or (b) possess limited communication skills in English. Students enroll in classes or are matched with a volunteer tutor for the purposes of instruction. Comings noted that in a recent program year, 48 percent of students were enrolled in basic literacy through intermediate level ABE instruction (grade level equivalent, 0 to 8), 20 percent in adult secondary education (grade level equivalent, 9 to 12), and 32 percent in English language instruction (English-language learners at student performance levels 0 to 8 or 9).

Comings described the great diversity of the student population. Adult education students include immigrants from many different countries and native-born Americans, men and women, 16-year-old high school dropouts and 70-year-old retirees, workers, welfare recipients, and prisoners. Some students have never been to school, while others have completed high school, and a few have college degrees. Most immigrant students do not have reading disabilities but many native-born students do. Students come to adult education programs to improve their English language, reading, writing, and math skills and to study for a high school equivalency credential. Students learning English typically fall into one of two groups: They either have a strong educational foundation in their native language, which may include advanced degrees, or they lack literacy in their native language. Every state, most programs, and even some individual classes exhibit this level of student diversity.

In program year 1999, the average expenditure per student (federal and matching funds combined) was $374, according to Bickerton. The average expenditure among the 10 states investing the most per student per year was $1,157, while among the 10 states spending the least, the average was $156 per student per year (DOEd, 2001b). In that same program year, students nationally received an average of 66 hours of instruction. This appears to have increased to an average of 86 hours per student in program year 2000. During the program year 1999, the average hours of instruction per student among the 10 states with the highest attendance was 106 hours, and it was only 31 hours for the 10 states with the lowest attendance. For program year 2000, the averages were 128 and 40 hours respectively for states with the highest and lowest attendance.

These low average numbers of attended hours are often not by design. Many adults are enrolled in class-based instruction. Many programs, particularly those for working adults, meet five or six hours per week. Classes targeted for unemployed adults can meet for 15 to 20 (or more) hours per week. According to the DOEd report, classes tend to run from 30 to 39 weeks in some programs (typical school year) and from 44 to 48 weeks in others (year-round). Hence, classes range from just under 200 hours per year to more than 800 hours, with most clustered at the lower end of the scale. The low average hours of attendance can be attributed to two factors. First, many students either drop out or "stop out" (leave and then return) because of other responsibilities. Adult education is not and cannot be the "number one priority" for most adults. Attending school is the primary responsibility for children. Adults, on the other hand, are raising families, working, and taking care of children and sick parents. As noted in a DOEd report, many students who want to continue in a program may drop out because of a change in work schedule or a crisis at home (Kaufman et al., 2000). Second, many students leave a program because they are not experiencing success. Although, this lack of success can be attributed to a number of factors, Bickerton said that dissatisfaction with the quality of adult education services, which are often undersupported, cannot be discounted.

3

Assessment and Test Design

Over the last 15 years, there has been a proliferation in the use of assessment for accountability purposes at the national, state, and local district level. Test results have been used as indices in making decisions about individual students, such as advancement from one grade to the next or graduation from high school. Test results have also been aggregated across individuals to make decisions about groups; they have been used to judge the quality of schools or to determine funding allotments within a district or state. Furthermore, test results have been aggregated to the state level and used as a tool to make comparisons among states. In short, tests have been used for many purposes (National Research Council [NRC], 1999b, 2001a).

At the workshop, Pamela Moss, a member of the joint committee that developed the *Standards for Educational and Psychological Testing* (American Educational Research Association [AERA] et al., 1999), observed that tests in educational settings are typically designed to fulfill one of three general purposes: (1) to provide diagnostic information, (2) to evaluate student progress, or (3) to evaluate programs (see NRC, 2001a for more information about the purposes of assessment). During the discussion about the purposes tests can serve in educational settings and in her overview of the *Standards*, Moss alluded to a number of measurement concepts. To assist readers not fully acquainted with measurement issues, the following background information about designing assessments is provided. Readers interested in more in-depth information on assessment design are referred to introductory measurement texts such as Millman and Greene (1993) and

Popham (1999, 2000). This chapter concludes with a discussion on the trade-offs to consider in designing and selecting assessments.

PURPOSES OF ASSESSMENT

An assessment that provides diagnostic information about a student's achievement level is considered a formative assessment; its intended purpose is to identify a student's areas of mastery and weaknesses in the content being studied in the classroom. Formative assessments can include classroom projects, teacher observation, written classwork, homework, and informal conversations with the students. Through formative assessment, the teacher gathers knowledge about what the student has learned, and that knowledge is used to facilitate instructional decisions about what content should be covered next. The results of formative assessments can provide feedback to individual students to help them focus their learning activities. To be of most benefit, formative assessment of student learning should be ongoing, closely aligned with instruction, and designed to support inferences about the students' developing competence with the content.

An assessment that evaluates student progress is a summative assessment; its intended purpose is to determine whether a student has obtained an established level of competency after completing a particular course of education—be it a classroom unit or 12 years of schooling. End-of-unit tests and letter grades are summative assessments. Summative assessments can also be large-scale assessments, such as the Massachusetts Comprehensive Assessment System (MCAS) or the General Educational Development (GED) exam.

Finally, assessments can be used to evaluate the overall performance of a particular program or group, such as a classroom, a school, a school district, or a state. For accountability, policy makers sometimes use data at the individual level, as well as data aggregated to the group level, to make judgments about the quality and effectiveness of educational programs and institutions. Examples of this kind of assessment include the Stanford 9, a standardized test that is designed to report scores at the individual level and is often aggregated to the group level, and the Maryland School Performance Assessment Program (MSPAP), which administers tests to samples of students and reports results for relevant groups. Results from assessments designed for program evaluation are used to support inferences about the overall performance of the group and often to make statements about the effectiveness of a given program.

Assessments can provide valuable information to help students, teachers, school administrators, and policy makers make a variety of decisions. Although a given assessment is generally designed to address a particular purpose, in practice that assessment is often used for multiple purposes. For instance, some state tests are used both to make decisions about performance of individuals and, when aggregated, to make judgments about the performance of a group (e.g., a classroom, school, or district).

ASSESSMENT DESIGN

According to the *Standards* (AERA et al., 1999), there are four phases of the test development process:

> (1) delineation of the purpose(s) of the test and the scope of the domain [content and skills] to be measured;
> (2) development and evaluation of the test specifications;
> (3) development, field testing, evaluation, and selection of items and scoring guides and procedures; and
> (4) assembly and evaluation of the test for operational use (p. 37).

This development process should be followed regardless of the kind of assessment being designed. Each aspect of test development is examined below.

Defining the Purpose and Identifying the Content and Skills to Be Assessed

A clear statement of purpose provides the test developer with a framework upon which to begin designing the assessment. In fact, in assessments such as the National Assessment of Educational Progress (NAEP), there is a document called the Framework that lays out the purpose of the assessments and defines the content to be measured. According to the *Standards*, the first step in test development is to define the purpose of the assessment and delineate the scope of the content and skills to be covered. When the assessments are to be used in educational settings, this process includes consideration of certain issues, such as how results will be used, the consequences—intended and unintended—of these uses, the articulated content standards, the material covered by the curriculum, and the ways in which students are to demonstrate mastery of the material.

The breadth of content and skill coverage included in assessments can vary considerably and will be guided by the intended purpose of the assessment and the inferences to be based on test results. For example, consider the GED, which students take to achieve the equivalent of a high school diploma. The purpose of the GED is to measure the skills associated with a high school education. The GED tests provide a standard measure of students' knowledge in mathematics, social studies, science, writing, literature, and the arts. But because a short series of tests (five content areas) cannot measure all the skills students should possess by high school graduation, the GED is designed to broadly measure knowledge and skills equivalent to those of graduating high school seniors, that is, the GED is normed against high school seniors who have been certified by their school registrars as having completed all the requirements for graduation. In contrast, consider an end-of-unit mathematics test. The test might be designed to indicate if students have mastered fractions as parts of a whole and as division, including familiar fractions such as halves, thirds, fourths, fifths, and tenths (National Council of Teachers of Mathematics, 2000). Here, the objective of the assessment is to measure a more narrowly defined content area with considerable depth. The results of the test tell the teacher which students are ready to move to the next mathematics topic and which need more instruction in this content area.

Another issue in defining the scope of the material covered by the assessment is to determine how test takers are to demonstrate their mastery of the content and skills. In educational measurement, there are two formats for collecting performance information about test takers: Selected-response items for which examinees select responses from several offered choices, or constructed-response items, for which examinees construct their own responses to test questions. Selected-response formats, such as multiple-choice, matching, or true-false, are suitable for many testing purposes and can easily and objectively be machine-scored. Other test purposes may be more effectively served by the constructed-response format. Short-answer items require a response of one or a few words. Extended-response formats may require the test taker to write a response of one or more sentences or paragraphs, design and carry out an investigation, or explain a solution to a practical problem that requires several steps. Most constructed-response items are scored by human scorers. Manual scoring of constructed-response items requires more time per item than selected-response items. Subjectivity is also an issue with scoring constructed-response items because scoring relies on judgments made by human scorers.[1]

[1]As mentioned in Chapter 1, several papers were commissioned after the workshop. The topic of a paper by Larry Frase will address how technology can facilitate scoring of constructed-response items. Please contact the DOEd to obtain the paper.

Included in the category of the constructed-response format are performance assessments. Performance assessments often seek to emulate the context or conditions in which the intended knowledge or skills would actually be applied, and they are characterized by the kind of response required from the test taker. Performance assessments generally require test takers to demonstrate their skills and content knowledge in settings that closely resemble real-life settings (AERA et al., 1999:41). One type of performance assessment is the standardized job or work sample. Job or work samples might include, for example, the assessment of a health care practitioner's skill in making an accurate diagnosis and recommending treatment for a defined medical condition, a manager's skill in articulating goals for an organization, or a student's proficiency in performing a science laboratory experiment. Another type of performance assessment is the portfolio. Portfolios are systematic collections of work or educational products usually created over time. A well-designed portfolio specifies the nature of the work that is to be put in the portfolio, which may include entries such as representative products, the best work of the test taker, or indicators of progress (AERA et al., 1999:42). For more information on developing portfolios, see LeMahieu, Gitomer, and Eresh (1995).

Whatever the format of the performance assessment, those who are involved in determining the scope of content and skills that will be addressed in the assessment usually include subject-matter experts, experienced practitioners, and other stakeholders. The process often includes consideration of the impact of the test on instruction because the material covered on the test may come to define the scope of what is taught in the classroom. Utilizing assessments to affect instruction at the classroom level can have both positive and negative consequences, depending on how well the knowledge and skills for the assessment match up with the knowledge and skills the instruction is supposed to cultivate.

Although portfolios and other types of performance assessment tasks provide a means for evaluating the skills that are not easily measured by selected-response items (e.g., performance in real-life situations), there are a number of attributes that really cannot be reliably assessed even with performance assessments. For instance, in discussing assessment of teachers, workshop speaker Mari Pearlman pointed out that qualities such as determination, perseverance, flexibility, and a sense of humor are critical for effective teaching, but the science of assessment cannot reliably define and measure these qualities and characteristics. Thus, while performance assessments offer a new approach to assessment, there are limits to what they can be expected to do. As Pearlman noted, "Our technical knowledge is not quite ready for some of the challenges presented by performance assessments."

Developing Test Specifications

Once the purpose of assessment and the scope of content and skill coverage have been determined, the test specifications can be developed. Test specifications are derived from the designated purpose of the test, and they provide a guide for developing multiple forms of the assessment. Test specifications can be considered the blueprint for the test (Mislevy, 1992), as they identify the number of items with specific characteristics to be included on each form. For instance, the test specifications might state the number of items measuring each content and skill area along with the numbers of each type of format (e.g., the number of selected-response and constructed-response items). Test specifications play a key role in enabling test forms to be constructed so that they cover similar skills in similar ways and produce results that are comparable.

Developing Items

The next stage of test construction is to develop items that measure the targeted content and skill areas laid out in the test specifications. The kinds of claims or inferences that are to be made about the knowledge or skills of interest must be considered in developing items. Items should be designed to provide salient evidence to support these claims.

Once items have been developed, they must undergo a number of reviews for appropriate content, clarity and lack of ambiguity, sensitivity to gender or cultural issues, and fairness (AERA et al., 1999:39). The quality of the items is usually ascertained through item review procedures and pilot testing. Often, a field test is developed and administered to a group of test takers who are representative of the target population. The field test helps determine some of the psychometric properties of the test items, such as an item's difficulty and its ability to discriminate among test takers with different skill levels, information that is used to identify appropriate and inappropriate items.

Assembling Test Forms

The final stage in test development is to assemble items into forms of the test or to identify an item pool for a computerized adaptive test. When the goal is to develop forms, it is important that each form meet the requirements of the test specifications. When the goal is to create an item pool for a computerized test, there should be enough items to address the test specifications. During the assembly of a test form, it is also important that scoring procedures be consistent with the purposes of the test and facilitate meaningful score interpretation. How the scores will be used determines the importance of psychometric characteristics of items in the test construction process.

DESIGNING PERFORMANCE ASSESSMENTS[2]

There are two critical components of a performance assessment: the task the student must carry out and the scoring guide, or *rubric*, used to judge the adequacy of the student's response. When test developers are designing performance tasks, they must first determine that examinees' skill levels can be assessed with a performance assessment task—that is, will the smaller number of items in a performance assessment be sufficient to base inferences about a student's mastery of the targeted content and skills? And for high-stakes assessments, will different forms of performance assessment lead to comparable decisions about students?

Scoring rubrics specify the criteria for evaluating performance. The scoring rubric describes the key features that must be included in a response to be awarded a specific score. It is useful to have samples of examinees' responses to demonstrate what is meant by the narrative description of each score level; these should include examples of responses scored at the upper and lower bounds for each level. The process for identifying the exemplar papers for each score level is called "range finding." Range finding is an important part of the rubric development process and involves determining for each score level on the rubric both the weakest and the strongest response. The scoring guide for a performance assessment is comprised of the rubric and example papers.

[2]The following text provides an overview of key aspects in developing and scoring performance assessments. It is not intended as a comprehensive guide. For additional information, see Popham, 2000.

The reliability of the scoring is an important issue. That is, it should not matter which scorer is rating a particular paper. With high reliability scoring, the ratings from different scorers on the same paper will be essentially the same. Ensuring high reliability requires carefully and unambiguously defined rubrics and extensive, careful training of scorers. To obtain a reliable score for each student, scoring procedures must indicate whether each critical dimension of the performance criteria is to be judged independently and scored separately or only an overall score is to be provided for each student. This determination will depend in part on the purposes of the assessment and costs. Often more detailed information is needed for formative assessments while fewer dimensions are scored for large-scale summative assessments. The reader is referred to Brennan (1983, 2001), Brennan and Johnson (1995), and Reckase (1995) for additional information on reliability in the context of performance assessments.

For scores on different forms of an assessment to be comparable, they must *mean* the same thing. This can be a special challenge with performance assessments. A statistical procedure called equating is typically used to make adjustments to scores derived from different test forms that are developed according to the same specifications. Equating requires carefully managed test construction, a data collection design, and statistical analyses. Equating works primarily because of the care that goes into ensuring that the tests measure essentially the same skills and with essentially the same degree of reliability.

Assembling equivalent forms is much more difficult for performance assessments than for selected-response tests because there are fewer tasks to work with, and each one requires some unique knowledge and skills. This leads to concerns that the same skill may not be measured on different versions of the performance assessments. Thus, rigorous statistical equating is usually not possible for performance assessments, and educators must use other methods for linking that have less stringent assumptions and provide lower degrees of comparability. Alternative linking methods (ways of making assessment results comparable across tests) are discussed in the next chapter.[3]

---

[3]The reader is referred to Kolen and Brennan (1995) for additional information about equating and to Green (1995) for a discussion of equating in the context of performance assessment.

CONSIDERATIONS IN CHOOSING AMONG ITEM FORMATS

There are benefits and issues associated with using either selected-response or constructed-response items in assessments. When selected-response format is used, more questions can be asked in a shorter period of time, scoring is faster and more straightforward, and it is easier to create comparable test forms. Because selected-response items can usually be answered quickly, many items covering several areas of the content can be administered in a relatively short period of time. Selected-response items are also machine-scoreable, and this allows for quicker and more objective scoring. The psychometric value of an objective scoring process is the reduction of error arising from variabilities in scoring procedures and thus higher score reliability. The costs of scoring tests with selected-response items are also generally fixed; it costs the same to score the test whether or not the items include maps or diagrams; the number of items on the assessment do not change the cost; and the price does not change from grade level to grade level (because issues like length of response are not relevant for selected-response). Because of these factors, the per-item cost of scoring tends to be minimal.

Workshop speakers discussed the advantages and disadvantages of different item formats. One disadvantage of selected-response items is that often they only assess test takers' recall and recognition skills and fail to capture higher-order thinking skills. Stephen Dunbar challenged this notion, saying that it is possible to write selected-response items that measure higher-order thinking skills. Writing high-quality selected-response items is difficult and requires skilled item writers, and writing selected-response items that assess more complex cognitive processes is even more difficult. Selected-response items are also susceptible to guessing. For example, with a binary-choice item such as a true-false question, examinees have a 50 percent chance of answering correctly whether or not they have mastered the material. There is also the perception that selected-response items often do not require application of the assessed skills and thus do not provide authentic information about a student's response to a real-life situation or problem.

An assessment that uses constructed-response items has the potential for obtaining richer information about the depth of student knowledge and understanding of a particular content area. Constructed-response items can certainly be written to tap students' higher-order thinking skills along with content knowledge. There is also a common perception (which is sometimes correct) that constructed-response items, especially performance assessment tasks, are more authentic because the tasks resemble real-world situations—they present real-world problems that require real-world problem solving.

Yet using constructed-response items raises both efficiency and economic issues. Constructed-response items usually require more time to answer; consequently, fewer items can be included on an assessment, and the coverage of content will be sparser than could be attained with selected-response items. In his presentation, Mark Reckase explained that 50 to 100 selected-response items can be administered to an adult in one hour, while no more than 10 performance assessments can be given in the same period of time. This leads to questions about content coverage and generalizability. With fewer tasks, it becomes difficult to generalize from performance on one sampling of tasks to another. A problem of some performance tasks is that they have low generalizability. That is, students may do well on some tasks but not on others and this is not a consequence of their skill level but simply because they are more engaged by some tasks then by others. A student may have the necessary background to be successful on a given task but may react to the specific context or other extraneous characteristics of the task. This reaction is referred to as a "person by task interaction" (Brennan and Johnson, 1995). When there are many tasks, as with selected-response questions, the lack of generalizability of a particular question is not a major issue, because results are averaged across many questions. When there are few questions, the "person by task interaction" becomes more important.

Scoring of constructed-response items, especially performance assessment tasks, is also difficult and costly. Dunbar cautioned that there is a per-item cost associated with developing and scoring performance assessment items, as rubrics have to be developed to evaluate the quality of students' responses. Although the development and scoring costs recur with both selected-response and constructed-response items, the recurring cost is considerably higher for tests that include performance assessment items. In addition, Dunbar reminded participants that the development of open-ended questions is not restricted to simply writing questions; it involves writing questions and anticipating answers. Although test developers attempt to design rubrics adaptive to many varied types of responses, unanticipated factors that arise during scoring often require the test developer to make adjustments, which can also mean additional scoring costs and retraining of scorers. Pearlman added, "There are many sad stories from the world of performance assessment where we forgot to think about scoring because we were seduced by the really enjoyable task of designing what people will do. That happens to be the most sexy part of all of this and is by far the most dangerous."

If the desire is to have scores that are comparable from one person to the next and from one testing occasion to the next, vigorous efforts need to be made to ensure consistent application of the scoring criteria across responses and across administrations. Scorers need extensive training so that they apply the scoring criteria similarly, and their scoring must be monitored throughout the process. Variability in the way the scoring criteria are applied can result when score descriptions are vague or scorers have biases not corrected during training. Some of the quality control procedures used with selected-response items, such as analysis of differential item functioning,[4] are more costly or difficult to carry out with constructed-response questions. There is also significant cost associated with training and payment of scorers. Reckase emphasized in his presentation that a defensible scoring procedure will require careful reader or scorer training.

Reckase said that constructed-response items take much longer to score than selected-response items. Even under optimal conditions he has found that only 10 performance assessment responses can be scored in one hour. This varies somewhat by the type of tasks and the skill level of the examinees. For example, responses of someone whose achievement level is at a second grade level are likely to be shorter and quicker to score than the responses of someone whose achievement level is at the tenth grade level.

Although these are serious issues for assessments designed to be formative and used for low-stakes purposes, they become crucial and raise fundamental questions of fairness in high-stakes tests in which results must be compared across tasks, raters, and programs. In either case, implementing performance assessments introduces additional measurement complexities and cost issues.

BALANCING TRADE-OFFS

Trade-offs are inevitable in designing an assessment and selecting item formats that both appropriately measure particular content and skill areas

---

[4]Differential item functioning occurs when examinees from different groups have differing probabilities of getting an item correct after being matched on ability (see Camilli and Shepard, 1994, or Holland and Wainer, 1993).

and serve the purpose of the assessment. In his closing comments, Reckase stressed that the kind of information that can be gathered from a set of items is limited by the information per unit of time. Multiple-choice items give many small bits of potentially unconnected information in a unit of time. Constructed-response items, particularly performance assessments, give fewer but larger and richer pieces of information, and they have the potential of providing more in-depth measurement of the students' knowledge within the content skill area.

ALIGNING TEST DESIGN WITH TEST PURPOSE

Over the last decade, assessment in adult education has generally been used to evaluate students' progress in various content areas. Most of the assessments in adult education programs are standardized tests (many of them norm-referenced)[5] that have been utilized by teachers to make placement decisions and determinations about student advancement through the program. In other programs, the tests have been used to measure advancement towards individual student goals such as learning to read or obtaining a GED. Requirements for NRS reporting, however, underscore the need to obtain information in a form in which it can be accumulated and compared at a national level. Not surprisingly, some of the differences in views about the purposes of assessment in adult education can be traced to differences in views about the purpose of adult education itself.

In his summary presentation, David Thissen shared his perception that workshop participants, like practitioners in the broader adult education arena, hold different beliefs about the fundamental purpose of adult education programs. Thissen heard some participants speak of the goal of adult education programs as aiding in the accomplishment of idiosyncratic and often functional goals that brought students to each program. In contrast, he said, other participants seemed to believe that the goal of adult education programs is to help each student make progress toward "becoming an educated person." In this view, the adult education programs are serving as an alternative to traditional K-12 school systems. According to Thissen, this point of view is implicitly expressed in the structure of the current NRS, which makes extensive use of difference scores[6] computed within a

---

[5]A norm-referenced test is used to ascertain an individual's status with respect to the performance of other individuals on the test (Popham, 2000).

[6]Difference scores are the change in scores from the pretest to the posttest.

TABLE 3-1 Purpose of the Adult Education Program

Purpose of the Assessment	Accomplishment of idiosyncratic goals	Progress toward becoming an educated person
Providing Diagnostic Information	A	B
Evaluating Student Progress	C	D
Evaluating the Program	E	F

SOURCE: Thissen (2002).

six-level scale that to some extent mirrors "progress" through elementary and secondary school systems in such subject areas as language and mathematics.

Thissen commented that participants also considered different purposes of assessment at different times in the workshop. In Table 3-1 the two broad purposes of adult education programs are crossed with the three traditional purposes of assessment in educational settings to form a display of six cells (labeled A through F). Each cell is defined below and grouped by purpose.

The first purpose of adult education to consider is the accomplishment of idiosyncratic goals—that is, the individual and often functional goals that bring each person to the program.

In Cell A the purpose of assessment is to provide diagnostic information about a student. An assessment for a student whose goal is to learn to read and write English might be a performance assessment designed to evaluate his or her proficiency in English. When the purpose of assessment changes to evaluating student progress (Cell C), an appropriate assessment might be one of the exams offered as a part of the Microsoft Certification program, which certifies an individual to be an MCP (Microsoft Certified Professional) or an MCSA (Microsoft Certified Systems Administrator) (see http://www.Microsoft.com/traincert/mcp/default.asp [April 29, 2002] for more information about these exams). Adult learners seek this kind of certification in order to qualify for a position or for career advancement. When the purpose of assessment is program evaluation, as in Cell E, the question becomes: Does the program help the student achieve his or her goals? An appropriate assessment might be a performance assessment designed at the local level for an adult education center to evaluate teachers' effectiveness.

If the purpose of adult education is the advancement of the student toward becoming an educated person (however that is defined), the kind of assessment changes for each assessment purpose. An assessment that meets this purpose of adult education and provides diagnostic information (Cell B) is the Degrees of Reading Power (DRP). DRP tests are holistic measures of students' comprehension of text. Test results are reported on a readability scale—the same scale that is used to measure the reading difficulty of printed material. By linking students' DRP test scores with the readability values of books, teachers are able to locate, assign, or recommend textbooks, literature, and popular titles of appropriate difficulty for their students. If the purpose of the assessment is to evaluate student progress (Cell D), assessments currently administered in adult education programs, such as TABE or CASAS, are appropriate. Finally, an assessment that serves the purpose of program evaluation (Cell F) is Maryland's MSPAP. The MSPAP is administered to third, fifth, and eighth graders, but scores are reported only at the school and district level, not at the level of the individual student.

The initiation of the NRS has led to the use of assessments for more than one purpose, and Thissen enumerated several concerns about this situation. For example, some largely multiple-choice tests that were originally designed to evaluate student progress, such as the assessments in Cell D, are now being used to provide program evaluation data (Cell F). As a test designer, Thissen's first question would be, "In which cell does the task fall?" The answer would guide decision making about assessment design. From his perspective as test designer, Thissen believes that the selection of the cell in which the problem lies is not a measurement issue. Rather, that selection needs to be made first, and the measurement issues and mechanics of developing an appropriate assessment can follow. Thus, sorting out the issues raised by purpose of programs and purposes of assessments, as illustrated in this table, is necessary for making sound decisions about the design and selection of adult education assessments.

4

Quality Standards for Performance Assessments

Standards for educational achievement have been developed that delineate the values and desired outcomes of educational programs in ways that are both transparent to stakeholders and provide guidance for curriculum development, instruction, and assessment. In addition, as described in Chapter 3, the measurement profession has developed a set of standards for the quality control of educational assessments. The *Standards for Educational and Psychological Testing* (American Educational Research Association [AERA] et al., 1999) provide a basis for evaluating the extent to which assessments reflect sound professional practice and are useful for their intended purposes.

This chapter highlights the purposes of assessment and the uses of assessment results that Pamela Moss presented in her overview of the *Standards.* The discussion then focuses on psychometric qualities examined in the *Standards* that must be considered in developing and implementing performance assessments. As mentioned in Chapter 3, Moss alluded to a number of measurement concepts during her workshop presentation. To assist readers who might be unfamiliar with the measurement issues included in the *Standards*, background information is provided on these issues.

USES FOR ASSESSMENT RESULTS

Assessments can be designed, developed, and used for different purposes, two of which—accountability and instruction—are particularly relevant to this report. As noted by several participants at the workshop, these two purposes are not always compatible, as they are concerned with different kinds of decisions and with collecting different kinds of information. Assessments for classroom instructional purposes are typically low stakes, that is, the decisions to be made are not major life-changing ones, relatively small numbers of individuals are involved, and incorrect decisions can be fairly easily corrected. Assessments for accountability, on the other hand, are usually high stakes: The viability of programs that affect large numbers of people may be at stake, resources are allocated on the basis of performance outcomes, and incorrect decisions regarding these resource allocations may take considerable time and effort to reverse—if, in fact, they *can* be reversed.

Assessment for instructional purposes is designed to facilitate instructional decisions, but instructional decision making is not the primary focus of assessments for accountability purposes. Assessments for instructional purposes may also include tasks that focus on what is meaningful to the teacher and the school or district administrator. But these particular tasks are not generally useful to external evaluators who want to make comparisons across districts or state programs. Hence, there is a trade-off in the kinds of information that can be gleaned from assessments for instructional purposes and assessments for accountability purposes. Assessments that are designed for instructional purposes need to be adaptable within programs and across distinct time points, while assessments for accountability purposes need to be comparable across programs or states.

Assessments for these two purposes also differ in the unit of analysis. When assessments are to be used for instructional purposes, the individual student is typically the unit of analysis. The resulting reported scores need to be sensitive to relatively small increments in individual achievement and to individual differences among students. For the purpose of accountability, the primary unit of analysis is likely to be larger (the class, the program, or the state). Assessments designed for this purpose need to be sensitive, not to individual differences among students but to differences in aggregate student achievement across groups of students (as measured by average achievement or by percentages of students scoring above some level). Because of these differences, the ways in which the quality standards apply to instructional and accountability assessments also differ.

While classroom instructional assessment is important in adult literacy programs, the primary concern of this workshop was with the development of useful performance assessments for the purpose of accountability across programs and across states because that is what the National Reporting System (NRS) requires. The discussion that follows focuses on issues raised by Moss in her presentation that are of concern in meeting quality standards in the context of high-stakes accountability assessment in adult education.

QUALITIES FOR PERFORMANCE ASSESSMENTS IN THE CONTEXT OF ADULT LITERACY

The *Standards* provide guidance for the development and use of assessments in general. However, discussion at the workshop focused on the ways in which these quality standards apply to, and are prioritized in, performance assessment, particularly in the context of adult education. The four qualities that were highlighted by Moss and others at the workshop are discussed in general terms and then with reference to performance assessment in adult education. These qualities are reliability, validity, fairness, and practicality.

Several points need to be kept in mind. First, the way these qualities are prioritized depends on the settings and purposes of the assessment. Thus, for a low-stakes classroom assessment for diagnosing students' areas of strength and weakness, concerns for authenticity and educational relevance may be more important than more technical considerations, such as reliability, generalizability, and comparability. For a high-stakes external accountability assessment, higher priority should be given to technical considerations. Much greater care will need to be taken, and more resources will need to be allocated, to ensure that assessments are reliable, valid, and comparable. Nevertheless, even though the qualities may be prioritized differently, *all* of them are relevant and need to be considered for every assessment.

Second, these qualities need to be considered at every stage of assessment development and use. Test publishers should not wait to determine how well assessments meet these quality standards until after they are in use. Rather, consideration of these standards should inform every decision that is made, from the beginning of test design to final decision making based on the assessment results.

Finally, there are costs associated with achieving quality standards in assessment. Differences in the priorities placed on the various quality standards will be reflected in the amounts and kinds of resources that are needed to achieve these standards. Thus, in any specific assessment situation, there are inevitable trade-offs in allocating resources so as to optimize the desired balance among the qualities.

RELIABILITY

Reliability is defined in the *Standards* (AERA et al., 1999:25) as "the consistency of . . . measurements when the testing procedure is repeated on a population of individuals or groups." Any assessment procedure consists of a number of different aspects, sometimes referred to as "facets of measurement." Facets of measurement include, for example, different tasks or items, different scorers, different administrative procedures, and different occasions when the assessment occurs. A reliable assessment is one that is consistent across these different facets of measurement. Inconsistencies across the different facets of measurement lead to measurement error or unreliability. A reliable assessment is also one that is relatively free of measurement error. The fundamental meaning of reliability is that a given test taker's score on an assessment should be essentially the same under different conditions—whether he or she is given one set of equivalent tasks or another, whether his or her responses are scored by one rater or another, whether testing occurs on one occasion or another. For additional information on reliability, the reader is referred to Brennan (2001), Feldt and Brennan (1993), National Research Council (NRC) (1999b), Popham (2000), and Thorndike and Hagen (1977). For a discussion on reliability in the context of performance assessment see Crocker and Algina (1986); Dunbar, Koretz and Hoover (1991); NRC (1997); and Shavelson, Baxter and Gao (1993). And for information on reliability in the context of portfolio assessment, see Reckase (1995). For a discussion of reliability in the context of language testing, see Bachman (1990), and Bachman and Palmer (1996).

Evaluating the Reliability of Performance Assessments

Evaluating the reliability of a given assessment requires development of a plan that identifies and addresses the specific issues of most concern. This plan will include both logical analysis and the collection of information or data. Multiple sources of evidence should be obtained, depending on the claims to be supported. Typically, the evaluation of reliability in performance assessments aims to answer five distinct but interrelated questions:

- What reliability issues are of concern in this assessment?
- What are the potential sources and kinds of error in this assessment?
- How reliable should scores from this assessment be?
- How can the reliability of the scores be estimated?
- How can reliability be increased?

Identifying Reliability Issues of Concern in Performance Assessment

In most educational settings, there are two major reliability issues of concern. One area of concern is the reliability of the scores from the assessments. Unreliable assessments, with large measurement errors, do not provide a basis for making valid score interpretations or reliable decisions. The second area of concern is the reliability of the decisions that will be made on the basis of the assessment results. These decisions may be about individual students (e.g., placement, achievement, advancement) or about programs (e.g., allocation of resources, hiring and retention of teachers). When assessments are used in decision making, errors of measurement can lead to incorrect decisions. Because these errors of measurement are not equally large across the score distribution (i.e., at every score level), the decisions that are based at the cut scores on different scales may differ in their reliability. The reader is referred to Anastasi (1988), Crocker and Algina (1986), and NRC (1999b) for additional discussion on the reliability of decisions based on test scores.

There are two types of incorrect decisions or classification errors. False positive classification errors occur when a student or a program has been mistakenly classified as having satisfied a given level of achievement. False negative classification errors occur when a student or program has been mistakenly classified as *not* having satisfied a given level of achievement. These classification errors have costs associated with them, but the costs may not be the same for false negative errors and false positive errors (Anastasi, 1988; NRC, 2001b). For example, what are the human and material resource costs of continuing to fund a program that is not meeting its objectives, even though, according to the assessment results, it appears to be performing very well? Alternatively, what is the cost of closing down a program that is, in fact, achieving its objectives, but, according to assessment standards, appears not to be? The potential for these and other types of errors must be considered and prioritized in determining acceptable reliability levels.

Identifying Potential Sources and Kinds of Error in Performance Assessment

Because most performance assessments include several different facets of measurement (e.g., tasks, forms, raters, occasions), a logical analysis of the potential sources of inconsistency or measurement error should be made in order to ascertain the kinds of data that need to be collected. In many performance assessments, the considerable variety of tasks that are presented make inconsistencies across tasks a potential source of measurement error (Brennan and Johnson, 1995; NRC, 1997). Another potential source of measurement error arises from inconsistencies in ratings. As mentioned previously, scoring performance assessment relies on human judgment. Inevitably, unless the individuals who are rating test takers' performances are well-trained, subjectivity will be a factor in the scoring process. Another source of inconsistency might be administrative procedures that differ across programs or states.

Determining How Reliable Scores from Given Performance Assessments Should Be

The level of reliability needed for any assessment will depend on two factors: the importance of the decisions to be made and the unit of analysis. Because most classroom assessment for instructional purposes is relatively low stakes, lower levels of reliability are considered acceptable. Hence, relatively few resources need to be expended in collecting reliability evidence for a low-stakes assessment. On the other hand, external assessments for accountability purposes, especially for individuals or small units, are relatively high stakes. Very high levels of reliability are needed when high-stakes decisions are based on assessment results. Considerable resources need to be expended to collect evidence to support claims of high reliability for these assessments.

When students' scores are used to make decisions about individual students, the reliability of these scores will need to be estimated. Estimating reliability is not a complex process, and appropriate procedures for this can be found in standard measurement textbooks (e.g., Crocker and Algina, 1986; Linn, Gronlund, and Davis, 1999; Nitko, 2001). Decisions about programs are usually based on the average scores of groups of students, rather than individuals. The reliability of these average scores will generally be better than that of individual scores because the errors of measurement will be averaged out across students. Thus, when decisions about programs are based on group average scores, higher levels of reliability can be expected than would be typically obtained from the individual scores upon which the group averages are based. Again, procedures are described in standard measurement texts.

Measurement error is only one type of error that arises when decisions are based on group averages. If the evaluation of program effectiveness is based on a sample of classes or programs rather than the entire population of such groups, the amount of sampling error must be considered. Sampling error can be considerable even when the group average scores are highly reliable. This error results from variation across groups or from year to year in terms of how well the groups represent the population from which they are sampled. If the groups do not adequately represent the population, the group average scores may be biased. Even if the groups represent the populations, it may be that the sample is such that there is a great deal of variability in the results. In either case, decisions based on these group average scores may be in error.

Gain Scores

Another issue arises when class or program average gain scores are used as an indicator of program effectiveness (AERA et al., 1999, Standard 13.17). "Gain score" refers to the change in scores from pretest to posttest. Even though the reliabilities of group gain scores might be expected to be larger than those obtained from individual gain scores, the psychometric literature has pointed out a dilemma concerning the reliability of change scores (see the discussion in Harris, 1963, for example).[1] One solution to the dilemma seems to be to focus on the accuracy of change measures, rather than on reliability coefficients in and of themselves. Nevertheless, the use of gain scores as indicators of change is a controversial issue in the measurement literature, and practitioners would be well advised to consult a measurement specialist or to review the technical literature on this subject (e.g., Zumbo, 1999) before making decisions based on gain scores.

---

[1]This is because the reliability of the change scores will be *highest* when the correlation between the pretest and posttest scores is *lowest*. However, if there is very little correlation between the pretest and posttest scores, one might question whether they are measuring the same ability. If they are not measuring the same ability, then it becomes very difficult to interpret the "change" in scores. This interpretation may be an artifact of overly restrictive assumptions in the derivation of change score reliability.

Estimating the Reliability of Scores

There is a wide range of well-defined approaches to estimating the reliability of assessments, both for individuals and for groups; these are discussed in general in the *Standards*, while detailed procedures can be found in measurement textbooks (e.g., Crocker and Algina, 1986; Linn et al., 1999; Nitko, 2001). These approaches include calculating reliability coefficients and standard errors of measurement based on classical test theory (e.g., test-retest, parallel forms, internal consistency), calculating generalizability and dependability coefficients based on generalizability theory (Brennan, 1983; Shavelson and Webb, 1991), calculating the criterion-referenced dependability and agreement indices (Crocker and Algina, 1986), and estimating information functions and standard errors based on item response theory (Hambleton, Swaminathan, and Rogers, 1991). In general, the specific approaches that should be used depend on the specific assessment situation and the unit of analysis and should address the potential sources of error that have been identified. No single approach will be appropriate for all situations. To determine the appropriate approach, consultation with professional measurement specialists is important.

Determining How Reliability Can Be Increased

When the estimates of reliability are not sufficient to support a particular inference of score use, this may be due to a number of factors. One set of factors has to do with the size and nature of the group of individuals on which the reliability estimates are based. If the groups used to collect data for estimating reliability either are too small or do not adequately represent the groups for which the assessments are intended, reliability estimates may be biased. If this is the case, the test developer or user will need to collect data from other larger and more representative groups. In most cases, however, low reliability can be traced directly to inadequate specifications in the design of the assessment or to failure to adhere to the design specifications in the creating and writing of assessment tasks. For this reason, the single most important step in ensuring acceptable levels of reliability is to design the assessment carefully and to adhere to this design throughout the test development process. As described in Chapter 3, the design process involves the following: clear and detailed descriptions of the abilities to be assessed and of the characteristics of test takers, clear and detailed task specifications for the assessment, clear and standardized administrative procedures, clear and understandable scoring procedures and criteria, and sufficient and effective training and monitoring of raters. The training of raters may have an additional benefit—it may tie in with professional development for teachers in adult education programs. When reliability estimates are low, each step in the development process should be revisited to identify potential causes and ways to increase reliability.

VALIDITY

Validity is defined in the *Standards* as "the degree to which evidence and theory support the interpretations of test scores entailed by proposed uses of tests" (AERA et al., 1999:9). Validity is a quality of the ways in which scores are interpreted and used; it is not a quality of the assessment itself. Validation is a process that "involves accumulating evidence to provide a sound scientific basis for the proposed score interpretations" (AERA et al., 1999:9). As with building support for claims about reliability, validation involves both the development of a logical argument and the collection of relevant evidence. The specific purposes for which the assessment is intended will determine the particular validation argument that is framed and the claims about score-based inferences and uses that are made in this argument. And the claims that are made in the validation argument will, in turn, determine the kinds of evidence that need to be collected. For more information, see, Messick (1989, 1995) and NRC (1999b). For an approach to framing a validation argument for language tests, see Bachman and Palmer (1996).

Three types of claims can be articulated in a validation argument. First, claims about score-based interpretations are derived from the explicit definition of the constructs, or abilities, to be measured; these claims argue that the test scores are reasonable indicators of these abilities, and they pertain to the construct validity of score interpretations. Second, claims about intended uses are twofold: they include the claim about construct validity and they argue that the construct or ability is relevant to the intended purpose, and that the assessment is useful for this purpose. Third, claims about the consequences of test use include an argument that the intended consequences of test use actually occur and that possible unintended or unfavorable consequences do not occur.

Many different kinds of evidence can be collected to support the claims made in the validation argument. The kinds of evidence that are relevant depend on the specific claims. No single type of evidence will be sufficient for supporting all kinds of claims or for supporting a given claim for all times, situations, and groups of test takers. The *Standards* discusses the following sources of evidence that support a validation argument:

- *Evidence based on test content.* Evidence that the test content is relevant to and representative of the content domain to be assessed can be collected through expert judgments and through logical and empirical analyses of assessment tasks and products.
- *Evidence based on response processes.* Evidence that the assessment task engages the processes entailed in the construct can be collected by observing test takers take assessment tasks and questioning them about the processes or strategies they employed while performing the assessment task, or by various kinds of electronic monitoring of test-taking performance.
- *Evidence based on internal structure.* Evidence that the observed relationships among the individual tasks or parts of the assessment are as specified in the construct definition can be collected through various kinds of quantitative analyses, including factor analysis and the investigation of dimensionality and differential item functioning. (See Comrey and Lee, 1992; Crocker and Algina, 1986; Cureton and D'Agostino, 1983; Gorsuch, 1983.)
- *Evidence based on relations to other variables.* Evidence that the scores are related to other indicators of the construct and are not related to other indicators of different constructs needs to be collected. The relationship between test scores and these other indicators provides criterion validity information. When the indicators reflect performance at the same time as the testing, this provides evidence of concurrent validity. When the indicators are gathered at some future time after the test, this provides evidence of predictive validity. When data for these analyses are collected, the accuracy and relevance of the indicators used in the analyses are of primary concern. An additional consideration in some situations is the extent to which evidence based on the relationship between test scores and other variables generalizes to another setting or use. That is, the evidence has been gathered for a particular group or setting, and it cannot be assumed that it will generalize to other groups or settings.
- *Evidence based on consequences of testing.* Evidence that the assessment will have beneficial outcomes can be collected by studies that follow test takers after the assessment or that investigate the impact of the assessment and the resulting decisions on the program, the education system, and society at large. Evidence about unintended consequences of assess-

ment can also be collected in this way. In this context, for example, accountability requirements may well impede program functioning, or they may conflict with client goals. Another kind of consequence that needs to be considered is impact on the educational processes—teaching and learning. One of the arguments made in support of performance assessments is that they are instructionally worthy, that is, they are worth teaching to (AERA et al., 1999:11-14).

Specific Validity Concerns in Performance Assessment in Adult Education

In addition to these general validity considerations, a number of specific concerns arise in the context of accountability assessment in adult education: (1) the comparability of assessments across programs and states, (2) the relative insensitivity of the reporting scales of the NRS to small gains, and (3) difficulties in interpreting gain scores.

Comparability of Accountability Assessments

If performance assessments are to be used to make comparisons across programs and states, these assessments must themselves be comparable. That is, if assessments are to be compared, an argument needs to be framed for claiming comparability, and evidence in support of this claim needs to be provided. Several general types of comparability and associated ways of demonstrating comparability of assessments have been discussed in the measurement literature (e.g., Linn, 1993; Mislevey, 1992; NRC, 1999c). These ways of making assessment results comparable are referred to as linking methods. The descriptions below draw especially on the presentation by Wendy Yen and are further described in Linn (1993), Mislevy (1992), and NRC (1999c).

- **Equating** is the most demanding and rigorous, and thus the most defensible, type of linking. It is reserved for situations in which two or more forms of a single test have been constructed according to the same blueprint. The forms adhere to the same test specifications, are of about the same difficulty and reliability, are given under the same standardized conditions, and are to be used for the same purposes. Scores and score interpretations from assessments that are equated can be used interchangeably so that it is a matter of indifference to the examinee which form or version of the test he or she receives. Equating is carried out routinely for new versions of large-scale standardized assessments.

- **Calibration** is a less rigorous type of linking. If two assessments have the same framework but different test specifications (including different lengths) and different statistical characteristics, then linking the scores for comparability is called calibration. The tests measure the same content and skills but do so with different levels of accuracy and different reliability. Unlike equating, which directly matches scores from different test forms, calibration relates scores from different versions of a test to a common frame of reference and thus links them indirectly. Calibration is commonly used in several situations. Sometimes a short form of a test is used for screening purposes, and its scores are calibrated with scores from the longer test. For example, calibration could be used to estimate, on the basis of a short assessment, the percentage of students in a program or in a state who would achieve a given standard if they were to take a longer, more reliable assessment. Sometimes tests designed for different grade levels are calibrated to a common scale, a process referred to as vertical equating.
- **Projection**, or prediction, is used to predict scores for one assessment based on those for another. There is no expectation that the content or constructs assessed on the two tests are similar, and the tests may have different levels of reliability. The statistical procedure for projection is regression analysis. It is important to note that projecting test A onto test B produces a different result from projecting test B onto test A. A limitation of projection is that the predictions that are obtained are highly dependent on the specific contexts and groups on which they are based. Additional studies to cross-validate these predictions are necessary if they are to be used with other groups of examinees because the relationships can change over time or in response to policy and instruction.
- **Statistical moderation** is used to align the scores from one assessment (test A) to scores from another assessment (test B). There is no expectation that tests A and B measure the same content or constructs, but the desire is to have scores that are in some sense comparable. Moderation is the process for aligning scores from two different assessments. With statistical moderation, the aligning process is based on some common assessment taken by both groups of examinees (test A and test B test takers).
- **Social moderation** is a nonstatistical approach to linking. Like statistical moderation, it is used when examinees have taken two different assessments, and the goal is to align the scores from the two assessments. Unlike statistical moderation, the basis for linking is the judgment of ex-

perts, common standards, and exemplars of performance that are aligned to these standards. Social moderation replaces the statistical and measurement requirements of the previous approaches with consensus among experts on common standards and on exemplars of performance. The resulting links (e.g., that a score of *a* on test A is roughly comparable to a score of *b* on test B) are only valid for making very general comparisons. The approach is often used to align students' ratings on performance assessment tasks. More relevant to this report is the use of social moderation to verify samples of student performances at various levels in the education system (school, district, state) and to provide an audit function for accountability.

Equating, calibration, or statistical moderation is typically used in high-stakes accountability systems. Social moderation is generally not considered adequate for assessments used for high-stakes accountability decisions.

The extent to which states' programs are aligned with the NRS standards is not known and was not the primary focus of this workshop. Further, although there may be states in which programs are consistent across the state, there is also the potential for lack of comparability of assessments across adult education programs and between states. This potential lack of comparability prompted workshop participants to raise a number of concerns, including the following:

- the extent to which different programs and states define and cover the domain of adult literacy and numeracy education in the same way;
- the consistency with which different programs and states are interpreting the NRS levels of proficiency;
- the consistency, across programs and across states, in the kinds of tasks that are being used in performance assessments for accountability purposes; and
- the extent to which these different kinds of assessments are aligned with the NRS standards.

These potential differences in the assessments used in adult education programs mean that none of the statistical procedures for linking described above are, by themselves, likely to be possible or appropriate. Social moderation, however, may provide a basis for framing an argument and supporting a claim about the comparability of assessments across programs and states.

Linn (1993) provides examples of uses of social moderation that are relevant to the context of accountability assessment in adult education, while Mislevy (1995) discusses approaches to linking, including social moderation, in the specific context of assessments of adult literacy. In his workshop presentation, Henry Braun gave two examples of what he calls "crosswalks" that use social moderation as an approach to linking scores from different assessments so they can support claims for comparability. He provided some specific suggestions for how this might be accomplished through the collaboration of various stakeholders, including publishers and state adult education departments.

All three experts call for certain elements to be present if the social moderation process is to gain acceptance among stakeholders. First, there must be an agreed-upon standard, or set of criteria, which provides the substantive basis for the moderation (i.e., for the process of aligning scores from different assessments). Second, there needs to be a pool of experts who are familiar with the content and context, the moderation procedure, and the criteria. Third, there must be a pool of exemplar student performances or products (benchmark performances) that the experts agree are aligned to different levels on the standard.

In the adult education context, the NRS can be considered the common standard, and the group of experts might include adult education teachers, program directors, state adult education administrators, test publishers, and external experts in the areas of adult education, literacy, and measurement. Braun suggested that the quality and comparability of the assessments could be improved by relying on test publishers' help. Publishers or states interested in developing assessments for adult education could be asked to state explicitly how the assessments relate to the framework, whether it is the NRS framework or the Equipped for the Future (EFF) framework, and to clearly document the measurement properties of their assessments.

Large Bands and Small Gains: The Relative Insensitivity of NRS Scales to Small Gains in Proficiency

The effectiveness of adult education programs is evaluated in terms of the percentages of students whose scores increase at least one NRS level from pretest to posttest. But, as Braun pointed out, two characteristics of the NRS scales create difficulties for their use in reporting gains in achievement. First, the NRS is essentially an ordinal scale[2] that breaks up what is, in fact, a continuum of proficiency into six levels that are not necessarily evenly spaced. An ordinal scale groups people into categories, and Braun cautioned that when this happens, there is always the possibility that some people will be grouped unfairly and others will be given an advantage by the grouping. In addition, although many students may make important gains in terms of their own individual learning goals, these gains may not move them from one NRS level to the next, and so they would be recorded as having made no gain. Indeed, given the breadth of the NRS scale intervals, the average gain may turn out to be zero unless many more scale points are differentiated within levels. Furthermore, the criterion for program effectiveness is a certain percentage of students who gain at least one NRS level, but many students are likely to achieve only relatively small gains in their limited time in adult education programs. This situation may result in individual programs devising ways in which to "game" the system; for example, they might admit or test only those students who are near the top of an NRS scale level. As Braun said, "We need to begin to develop some serious models for continuous improvement so we avoid the rigidity of a given system and the inevitable gamesmanship that would then be played out in order to try to beat the system."

Braun raised another complicating issue: The NRS educational functioning levels are not unidimensional but are defined in terms of many skill areas (literacy, reading, writing, numeracy, functional and workplace). Although a student might make excellent gains in one area, if he or she makes less impressive gains in the area that was lowest at intake, the student cannot increase a functioning level according to the DOEd guidelines (2001a). Braun noted that the levels can also affect program evaluation. For example, because of a program's particular resources and teaching expertise or the particular needs of its clientele, it may do an excellent job at teaching reading, but the students' overall progress is not sufficient to move them from one NRS level to the next. As a result, the program would receive no credit for its students' impressive gains in reading.

---

[2]An ordinal scale provides a simple rank ordering of categories. There is no assumption that the categories are evenly spaced (i.e., what it takes to move from one category to the next is the same across categories). For instance, in the NRS it may require more improvement in achievement to move from the low intermediate basic education level to the next level (high intermediate basic education level) than to move from the beginning adult basic education (ABE) literacy level to the next level (beginning basic education level).

An additional concern is that the kinds of performance assessments that might be envisioned may be even less sensitive to tracking small developmental increments than some assessments already being used. Performance assessment tasks tend to be more cognitively demanding, educationally relevant, and authentic to real-life situations, which means they are not usually designed to focus either on small increments or on the component skills and abilities that may contribute to successful performance on the task as a whole.

Difficulties in Interpreting Gain Scores Due to the Effects of Instruction

Some of the measurement issues in using gain scores as indicators of student progress have been discussed above. In addition to these measurement issues, a number of other problems make it difficult to attribute score gains to the effects of the adult education program. Braun explained that the fundamental problem is that there are a number of factors in the students' environment, other than the program itself, which might contribute to their gains on assessments. Most students who are English-language learners are living in an environment in which they are surrounded by English. Many are also working at jobs where they are exposed to materials in English and required to process both written language and numerical information in English. The amount of this exposure varies greatly from student to student and from program to program. Thus, it is difficult to know the extent to which observed gain scores are due to the program rather than to various environmental factors.

To rigorously study the effects of adult education on literacy, it would be necessary to distinguish its effects from those of the environment. Furthermore, differences in the home environments of students, as well as any preexisting individual differences in students as they enter an adult education program, would need to be controlled. This would mean that an experiment would be conducted in which individuals from the adult population were selected at random, and some were chosen at random to be placed in adult education classes, while the others (the comparison group) would merely continue with their lives and not pursue adult education. Although a few experimental studies have been conducted (St. Pierre et al., 1995), there are obvious reasons—practical, pedagogical, and ethical—for not implementing this kind of experimental control. First, students in adult education programs are largely self-selected, and it would be impractical to try to obtain a random sample of adults to attend adult education classes. Second, if the adult education classes included students who were randomly selected rather than people who had chosen to take the classes, there would be major consequences for the ways in which the adult education classes were taught. Finally, denying access to adult education to the individuals in the comparison group would raise serious ethical questions about equal access to the benefits of our education system. Thus, it is neither possible nor desirable to conduct studies in educational settings with the level of experimental control expected in a laboratory. This lack of control makes it extremely difficult to distinguish between the effects of the adult education program and the effects of the environment.[3]

FAIRNESS

The *Standards* discusses four aspects of fairness: (1) lack of bias, (2) equitable treatment in the testing process, (3) equality in outcomes of testing, and (4) opportunity to learn (AERA et al., 1999:74-76).

Lack of Bias

The *Standards* defines bias as occurring when scores have different meanings for different groups of test takers, and these differences are due to deficiencies in the test itself or in the way it is used (AERA et al., 1999:74). Bias may be associated with the inappropriate selection of test content; for example, the content of the assessment may favor students with prior knowledge or may not be representative of the curricular framework upon which it is based (Cole and Moss, 1993; NRC, 1999b). Potential sources of bias can be identified and minimized in a variety of ways including: (1) judgmental review by content experts, and (2) statistical analyses to identify differential functioning of individual items or tasks or to detect systematic differences in performance across different groups of test takers.

---

[3]While this is true in most states, some states (e.g., Massachusetts) have established controls on the number of students programs can enroll, based on the level of resources available to each program. This is meant to ensure that the students who are enrolled can benefit from the full range of services and supports deemed essential to their success ("opportunity to learn"). These states often have long waiting lists, e.g., nine months to two years for ESOL classes in larger cities in Massachusetts. Hence, there may be a possibility for achieving control groups that are very nearly equivalent.

Equitable Treatment in the Testing Process

All test takers should be given a comparable opportunity to demonstrate their level on the skills and knowledge measured by the assessment (NRC, 1999b). In most cases, standardization of assessments and administrative procedures will help ensure this. However, some aspects of the assessment may pose a particular challenge to some groups of test takers, such as those with a disability or those whose native language is not English. In these cases, specific accommodations, or modifications in the standardized assessment procedures, may result in more useful assessments. All test takers need to be given equal opportunity to prepare for and familiarize themselves with the assessment and assessment procedures. Finally, the reporting of assessment results needs to be accurate and informative, and treated confidentially, for all test takers.

Equality in Outcomes of Testing

Unequal performance across different population groups on a given assessment is not necessarily the result of unfair assessment. Differential test performance across groups may, in fact, be due to true group differences in the skills and knowledge being assessed; the assessment simply reflects these differences. Alternatively, differential group performances may reflect bias in the assessment. When differences occur, there should be heightened scrutiny of the test content, procedures, and reporting (NRC, 1999b). If there is strong evidence that the assessment is free of bias and that all test takers have been given fair treatment in the assessment process, then conditions for fairness have been met. The reader is referred to Bond (1995) and Cole and Moss (1993) for additional information on bias and fairness in testing in general and to Kunnan (2000) for discussions of fairness in language testing.

Opportunity to Learn

In educational settings, many assessments are intended to evaluate how well students have mastered material that has been covered in formal instruction. If some test takers have not had an adequate opportunity to learn these instructional objectives, they are likely to get low scores. These low scores differ in meaning from low scores that result from a student's having had the opportunity to learn and having failed to learn. Interpreting both types of low scores as if they mean the same thing is fundamentally unfair. In the context of adult literacy, where there are extreme variations in the amount of time individual students attend class (e.g., 31 hours per student per year in the 10 states with the lowest average and up to 106 hours per student among the 10 states with the highest average), the fairness of using assessments that assume attendance over a full course of study becomes a crucial question.

Three problematic issues need to be considered with respect to this conception of fairness. First, opportunity to learn is a matter of degree. In addition, in order to measure some outcomes, it may be necessary to present students with new material. Second, even though the assessment may be based on a well-defined curricular content domain, it will nonetheless be only a sample of the domain. It may not be possible to determine the exact content coverage of a student's assessment. Finally, in many situations, it is important to ensure that any credentials awarded reflect a given level of proficiency or capability.

In the context of adult literacy assessment, the issues discussed above—comparability of assessments, insensitivity of the NRS functioning levels to small increments in learning, and the use of gain scores—are also fairness issues. If different assessments are used in different programs and different states, one may well question whether they favor some test takers over others, and whether all test takers are given comparable treatment in the testing process. If gain scores are used to evaluate program effectiveness, the relative insensitivity of the NRS levels may be unfair to students and programs that are making progress within but not across these levels.

Several of the workshop participants pointed out that issues of fairness, as with validity, need to be addressed from the very beginning of test design and development. In addition, there is considerable potential for professional development in educating teachers to the fact that fairness includes making learners aware of the kinds of assessments they will be encountering and ensuring that these assessments are aligned with their instructional objectives.

PRACTICALITY

Finally, an overriding quality that needs to be considered is practicality or feasibility. Attaining each of the above quality standards in any assessment carries with it certain costs or required resources. To the extent that the resources are available for the design, development, and use of an assessment, the assessment can be said to be practical or feasible. Practicality concerns the adequacy of resources and how these are allocated in the design, development, and use of assessments. Resources to be considered are human resources, material resources, and time. Human resources are test designers, test writers, scorers, test administrators, data analysts, and clerical support. Material resources are space (rooms for test development and test administration), equipment (word processors, tape and video recorders, computers, scoring machines), and materials (paper, pictures, audio- and videotapes or disks, library resources). Time resources are the time that is available for the design, development, pilot testing, and other aspects of assessment development; assessment time (time available to administer the assessment); and scoring and reporting time. Obviously, all these resources have cost implications as well.

In most assessment situations, these resources will not be unlimited. Thus, there will be inevitable trade-offs in balancing the quality standards discussed above with what is feasible with the available resources. Braun discussed a trade-off between validity and efficiency in the design of performance assessments. There may be a gain in validity because of better construct representation, as well as authenticity and more useful information. However, there is a cost for this in terms of the expense of developing and scoring the assessment, the amount of testing time required, and lower levels of reliability. The reader is referred to Bachman and Palmer (1996) for a discussion of issues in assessing practicality and balancing the qualities of assessments in language tests.

Bob Bickerton spoke about practicality issues in the adult education environment. He noted that the limited hours that many ABE students attend class have a direct impact on the practicality of obtaining the desired gains in scores for a population that is unlikely to persist long enough to be posttested and, even if they do, are unlikely to show a gain as measured by the NRS. John Comings said his research indicated that for a student to achieve a 75 percent likelihood of making a one grade level equivalent or one student performance level gain, he or she would have to receive 150 hours of instruction (Comings, Sum, and Uvin, 2000). Bickerton added that Massachusetts has calculated that it takes an average of 130 to 160 hours to complete one grade level equivalent or student performance level (see SMARTT ABE http://www.doe.mass.edu/acls [April 29, 2002]). The NRS defines six ABE levels and six ESOL levels. A comparison of the NRS levels with currently available standardized tests indicates that each NRS level spans approximately two grade level equivalents or student performance levels. Bickerton noted that it could take up to double the 150 hours mentioned above to complete one NRS level for students who, on average, are receiving instruction for a total of just 66 to 86 hours (DOEd, 2001c). These issues of practicality or feasibility are of particular concern in the development and use of performance assessments in adult education. Chapters 5 and 6 discuss these issues in greater detail.

5

Developing Performance Assessments for the National Reporting System

Many in the adult education community believe that performance assessments are more congruent with the goals and real-life scenarios of adult learners and allow for broader measurement of adult learners' skills than standardized multiple-choice tests, such as CASAS and TABE (described in Chapter 2). Specifically, many believe that performance assessment tasks provide students with better opportunity to demonstrate their knowledge of the content by producing or constructing a response to an item or task, rather than simply selecting a response from available options. (As Myrna Manly and Stephen Dunbar noted, this contrast between performance assessments and multiple-choice assessments is overly stark. While performance assessments do indeed make it possible to gather rich evidence about students by presenting them with more complex situations, thoughtfully constructed multiple-choice tests can engage higher-order thinking, and poorly constructed performance assessments can obfuscate students' achievement with demands for irrelevant knowledge.) The trade-off of using performance assessment tasks instead of selected-response tasks is that considerably fewer questions can be asked in the same period of time. This leads to issues about limitations of performance assessments to represent the scope of the content and skills covered on the assessments.

ACHIEVING DOMAIN COVERAGE

Several approaches for achieving domain coverage were suggested during the workshop. Two of these are examined in this section: the critical indicator approach and the domain sampling approach.

The Critical Indicator Approach

Mark Reckase described the critical indicator approach. With this approach, specific skills are identified as more important than others in a particular content area; then tasks are designed to assess those critical skills. The approach rests on the assumptions that can be made about a student's mastery of the targeted set of content and skills based on his or her ability to successfully complete the critical tasks. If the student can perform the critical tasks, it is reasonable to infer that he or she possesses the capability to perform other less critical tasks that assess similar content and skills.

Reckase said that identifying the critical tasks and knowledge that indicate competence in a given content and skill area is the most important component of the critical indicator approach; it requires an in-depth understanding of the domain to be accessed. If the assessment tasks are not on target, the results will not provide useful information. The development of scoring procedures is consistent with the procedures for performance assessments discussed in Chapter 3. It includes conducting range-finding activities with initial products to determine the number of score levels that can be supported, and developing rater evaluation and training materials.

Reckase offered several examples of particular skills in adult education that might be critical tasks: A critical writing task would be creating a multi-paragraph memo on job-related tasks, and a critical mathematics task would be a business application of mathematics. Identifying critical reading tasks would entail identifying types of texts that can be used to show accomplishment of the reading goals related to understanding text. The inference is that if an individual can read and understand a complex type of text, then he or she can comprehend other less complex texts. The process of identifying critical tasks requires consideration of scoring procedures. Specifically, it is important that the task allows individuals at different skill levels to demonstrate their proficiency. Further, it is important to ensure that a rating scale can be developed that allows responses at multiple skill levels to be scored.

Once critical indicators are identified, the time requirement for assessment is low. By focusing on critical skills and using a short screening pretest to assign performance tasks, this strategy attempts to use what is known about the structure of the domain and what is learned about the functioning level of the examinee to administer only those tasks most likely to be informative for that particular person. A disadvantage of this approach is that inferences about mastery of the targeted set of content and skills are based on a limited sampling of behavior. In addition, those who are developing the assessment must agree on the overall domain, have a deep understanding of the skills and knowledge required, and be able to select the critical tasks in each content area.

The Domain Sampling Approach

Another alternative for selecting tasks is to sample from the domain that is the targeted set of content and skills in a given subject area. In this approach, a large number of tasks are developed that represent all of the content and skills in the particular subject area. For a given test administration, a smaller number of tasks are randomly selected and administered to the student. Thus, any given form of the assessment is assumed to be a representative sample of the skills and knowledge included in the domain. The idea is that if a student can do well on an assessment of a representative sample of the skills and knowledge in a content area, then it is appropriate to infer that he or she possesses mastery of the domain. In this approach, the goal of assessment development is to produce an instrument that contains tasks that are an appropriate sample of a domain. Ideally, a content framework would be translated into specifications that clearly delimit the types of performance items included in the domain. Test developers would then produce many items that represent the domain, and forms would be developed by sampling from the set of items.

A primary benefit of this approach is its familiarity; it draws on procedures usually used to develop a pool of assessment tasks to assess the range of knowledge and skills in a content domain. The targeted knowledge and skills are first mapped out; then tasks are created that not only assess that knowledge but further specify exactly what the student is expected to learn. This step has the added benefit of educating students and teachers as to what is covered by the test. As with the critical indicator approach, the test developers must agree on the range of tasks that represent the skills and knowledge of the content area, and they must be confident that these tasks are representative.

Reckase said that there are two disadvantages to the domain sampling approach. First, it takes a substantial amount of time to obtain good domain coverage, a problem not unique to adult education. A second issue that may be more serious in adult education is the apparent lack of consensus on a definition of the domain. If different states or different adult education programs disagree on what the domain includes, sampling in the same way from the same pool of tasks will not adequately meet the purposes of all the programs. Constructing large and comprehensive pools of tasks, from which programs would specify areas of interest and construct their own sampling plans, is one possible solution to this problem. Yet utilizing this option increases the difficulty of both constructing assessments and comparing results across states and programs.

HOW STUDENTS DEMONSTRATE PROFICIENCY

For those states and local programs that want to use performance assessments to measure students' proficiency, there are several options. These options were proposed as ways to adhere to the NRS requirements and to assess a variety of content areas.

Types of Performance Assessments

Performance assessments use different modes for students to provide responses to questions. One mode calls for examinees to actively demonstrate their responses. Another mode makes use of a written response, while others involve students constructing portfolios of their work.

Performance Tasks

A performance task requires examinees to actively demonstrate their skills. An example of a numeracy task that uses math to solve a realistic problem follows. For example, one such task might involve a consumer math problem in which students are asked to plan a trip to the supermarket. They have a certain amount of money to spend and must generate a shopping list for the week. Using a simulated newspaper ad or worksheet, they must find the prices for each item on their list and calculate the total bill. This is one of many possible examples of authentic performance assessment tasks that assess numeracy skills. As Myrna Manly commented, context is a key feature that increases the authenticity of the task.

Written Scenarios

In a written scenario, a type of on-demand writing task, students are required to write a response to an oral or written prompt (the question and tasks proposed to the examinee). This performance assessment task requires that students apply previous knowledge and pose solutions to realistic problems. The responses may vary in length and usually have several parts. The written scenario has a title, a prompt, and instructions to the student on the specific questions that he or she must address and the aspects of the content that should be included. The evaluation criteria should also be included so that the students know which skills will be evaluated in their responses. An example of a written scenario appears below:

> *Scenario*: Ben's goal is to find work as a sales associate for a department store. He has never worked in a department store before but he feels that he has good interpersonal skills. Ben's strategy for finding a job is to look at the job ads in the paper every week and send his resume in response to the ads. It has been two months and Ben has not yet found a job or even been asked for a job interview. Because Ben is your friend, he comes to you for advice on seeking work as a sales associate.
>
> *Instructions*: What feedback would you give to Ben on his strategy for finding a job as a sales associate? Specifically, describe two strategies you think that Ben should consider to be more effective in seeking work as a sales associate. Explain how you would present these strategies to Ben.
>
> *Your response will be evaluated on your ability to*:
> - plan (evaluate a plan's effectiveness in achieving goals);
> - solve problems and make decisions (generate strategies of options for effective action);
> - convey ideas in writing;
> - guide others (Ananda, 2000:10).

Written scenarios are easy to develop and administer; they can be modified for either a short or long response; and they can be administered in either individual or group format. At the same time, as Mari Pearlman pointed out, substantial effort is required to design a system for evaluating responses to written scenarios. Shared rubrics, illustrated by examples of performances and ratings that are linked to scoring levels, would increase the comparability of results from this kind of task.

Portfolio Assessment

The type of performance assessment that received the most attention at the workshop was the portfolio task. As discussed in Chapter 3, a portfolio is a systematic collection of work or educational products created over a certain period of time. The workshop speakers believed that the portfolio was a feasible assessment vehicle for either domain coverage approach discussed above. Less clear is how portfolio assessment would fit into the pretest/posttest paradigm of the NRS. Reckase suggested the use of structured portfolios in which the student would have to follow a prescribed table of contents to create the portfolio; this would ensure some commonality of evidence across examinees. According to Reckase, the table of contents would be useful in narrowing the scope of content coverage and in ensuring that similar information is collected from students from one testing occasion to the next. A fixed menu of options would also allow for the advance development of scoring rubrics for the kinds of assessments included in the table of contents. A menu of options can be developed through either method of achieving domain coverage or in some other way. Developing structured scoring procedures and rubrics is important for maintaining consistency in the scoring process and for enabling comparisons of students' work from one testing occasion to another.

For the menu to be useful, each task or work sample description would have to be defined clearly enough to be specific about the kinds of work students should include in the structured portfolio. Using the menu, a student and teacher could select the task that most appropriately matches the student's personal and instructional goals. Reckase envisioned a one-page description of the work sample that would be generic enough for the student and teacher to adapt to their stated goal. He also stressed the importance for both the student and the teacher of understanding what constitutes acceptable and unacceptable entries. He highlighted the time, cost, and difficulty of developing scoring procedures for portfolios but said that it can be done (National Board for Professional Teaching Standards,

2000; Reckase, 1995; Reckase and Welch, 1999). Reckase also emphasized how important competent and well-trained raters are to the success of this process.

Reckase provided an example of a portfolio menu for English Language Arts. Some of the tasks and the work sample description include the following:

- analysis/evaluation (analyze or evaluate different aspects or parts of a subject, object, or idea);
- explanatory writing (explain a process or concept to another person through writing);
- proposing a solution (define a problem and offer a plausible solution); and
- research/investigative writing (research a subject, gather and organize material, and present it clearly with well-documented sources).

At the end of the instructional period, the student and teacher would select the best piece of work to be evaluated for each relevant task. Reckase recommended producing a handbook for students and teachers that describes the scoring procedures and the rubric and provides examples of work that would fit into the different score categories. He suggested that a minimum of five entries of student work would be needed in a portfolio to obtain a reliable student score on a particular content area.

Reckase commented that although portfolios can be a very effective tool for evaluating growth, they do present some complications. For a structured portfolio to be used as part of the assessment system, instructors must agree on the content and types of activities that a student should include. It is difficult to develop scoring procedures that are reliable enough to enable the comparison of different work products by different students. Specifically, the cross-task generalizability of performance measures can be weak. This means that a person's performance may depend on the task he or she is given. Furthermore, portfolios often include products of both successful and unsuccessful performance on different tasks. Thus, the scoring process needs to include ways to handle portfolios in which students do well on one task and not as well on others—that is, their performance across tasks is uneven. Reckase noted that these factors demonstrate that achieving comparability of students' performance and program effectiveness is difficult. The fact that different students' portfolio entries are tailored to the substance and the levels they are working on means that each student's performance is more relevant to him or her individually and less commensurate with those of other students. As a result, there is more judgment involved in mapping performances into a common framework (such as the NRS levels), and a greater burden is placed on the need to achieve consistency of evaluations across students, over time, and among programs.

Reckase emphasized the need for scorers who have knowledge of the content and skill area being assessed and who have gone through a thorough training process. Scoring guides should be developed for the training process, and they should include rating points with clear descriptions and exemplar papers. This is especially critical if the assessment system is to provide information about the six levels of performance prescribed in the NRS. There must also be a provision for monitoring the quality of portfolio scoring and for refresher training. These caveats do not apply only to the assessment of portfolios but to other performance assessments as well. One discussant cautioned that developing performance assessments that meet technical standards is challenging. He pointed out that earlier K-12 education reform efforts in Vermont and Kentucky were unsuccessful in their attempts to use portfolio assessment as the foundation for their high-stakes accountability systems. (See Koretz, Stetcher, Klein and McCaffrey, 1994, for more information.)

WAYS TO IMPROVE EFFICIENCY

Multi-Stage Testing

One suggestion that was promoted by Wendy Yen and others is multi-stage testing. In multi-stage testing, students take an initial "routing test" or locator test. The locator test is a short, broad measure of the content that provides an initial estimate of the students' level of skills. On the basis of their performance on the locator test, students are routed to a test approximately at their skill level. The second-stage tests are of varying levels of difficulty; they are longer and provide a more precise estimate of the students' skill level. Multi-level testing can be performed with either paper-and-pencil tests or computer.

Computerized Testing

The use of computerized testing can greatly improve the testing process, making it more efficient and flexible. With computer-based testing, a paper-and-pencil test is converted to a computer-administered test. Questions are presented to examinees in the same sequence as on the paper-and-pencil test, and the examinees choose their answer selections in the same manner as they would on a paper-and-pencil test. Once an examinee finishes responding to all the questions, the test is scored.

Another more technically sophisticated form of computer-administered test is the computerized adaptive test (CAT). CATs rely on programmed algorithms that use an examinee's response to a given question to select the next question. The difficulty level of the administered items is adapted to the skill level of the examinee. Thus, test takers spend less time answering questions that are too hard or too easy for them. CATs greatly increase test efficiency because examinees do not have to answer all the questions. The programmed algorithm continues presenting items to the examinee until the examinee's skill level can be estimated with sufficient precision. Computer-adaptive testing is a special type of multi-stage testing that exploits the capability of the computer in the presentation of questions and in scoring. Ronald Hambleton explained that computer-adaptive testing makes it possible to target the assessment to the student's ability, build in flexibility in scheduling tests, and increase test security as well. (Additional information on computer-adaptive testing can be found in Wainer et al., 2000.)

Although the technology available for computer-adaptive testing makes it most feasible for use with multiple-choice test items, CAT has also been used to develop simulations of real-life situations, using selected-response items, which are included on licensure exams for doctors and architects. According to Hambleton, the computer technology for automated scoring is advancing rapidly. A number of workshop participants described examples of performance tasks that use automatic scoring, such as the simulation-based networking tasks used in the Microsoft certification exams[1] and the computerized patient management problems used in the National Board of Medical Examiners' licensing examination for physicians.[2]

Hambleton said that the positive features of computer-based testing for adult education include: (1) flexibility in scheduling tests (participants can take tests when they are ready and without the aid of a test administra-

---

[1]Website: http://www.microsoft.com/traincert/mcp. [March 28, 2002]

[2]Website: http://www.usmle.org/. [May 14, 2002]

tor; consequently instructors are not overwhelmed by testing responsibilities), and (2) increased test security (the tests are in the computer and not available in paper form, and new test designs and item formats are possible). CAT permits the targeting of assessments to the ability levels of the examinees. In adult education, which has a wide range of abilities among students, targeting the difficulty of the test to each student would be a major advantage—students would experience less frustration, measurement precision could be increased, and testing time could be shortened.

Presenters agreed that the introduction of computer technology into assessment practices provides several advantages for adult education: More valid assessments can be developed; assessments can be individualized; flexibility in test scheduling is possible; feedback and scoring of students can be immediate; and testing time can be minimized. Computer technology is also useful in addressing psychometric issues such as scaling and measuring a large continuum of skill levels; it provides more options for analyzing the data (scaling, calibration), and it allows administration across sites and localities. Hambleton and others cautioned, however, that computer technology will require a large item bank; items will still need to be field-tested and calibrated; and the initial cost of computers is substantial.

Item Sampling: Maryland School Performance Assessment Program

In the early 1990s, the state of Maryland implemented an innovative and challenging educational reform program that held schools, not students, accountable for student performance. The reform program dramatically altered Maryland's student assessment program and led to the design of an assessment system that uses performance-based assessments for school evaluation. The Maryland School Performance Assessment Program (MSPAP) is administered annually to third, fifth, and eighth graders. It includes assessments in reading, writing, language usage, mathematics, science, and social studies. All the assessment tasks are integrated across the content and are authentic in that students respond to queries based on problems solved during the examination process. According to Mark Moody, the assessment was designed to embody sound instructional practices and to represent good principles of instruction and—most important—to obtain reliable school-level scores (because the focus is on program evaluation), rather than accurate scores for individual students (thereby reducing the burden on individual students). The model is described here for its instructional purposes even though it would not fulfill the NRS requirements.

MSPAP is a criterion-referenced assessment[3] based on the Maryland learning outcomes. The MSPAP uses matrix sampling so that students are assessed on different aspects of the content, with no student completing all items on the assessment. Aside from the greater complexity of administering such an assessment, this design offers measurement advantages for Maryland's objectives of assessing schools over a very broad range of content while minimizing individual student testing burden.

According to Moody, there are several advantages to Maryland's performance-based assessments. State policy makers believe that MSPAP is a test worth teaching to. According to Moody, "It embodies the spirit of good instruction." Maryland has also found that the assessment has face validity[4] with constituents, it provides models of performance opportunities, and it has provided a rich source of data for school improvement.

But the MSPAP also has several disadvantages. The assessment is complex, it is expensive, and it does not provide individual student results. The cycle for creating an edition of the test is 30 months, and about 24 months of that cycle are spent writing the items. Moody reported that it is challenging to find authentic materials and readings, and the developers encounter copyright issues in what material can be used and how it can be used. The expense of the MSPAP is calculated at about $60 per student for development, scoring, and reporting, and this does not include expenses associated with test administration time. Administering performance assessment tasks can be more time- and labor-intensive than administering other types of assessments. Approximately 180,000 students are tested yearly. Finally, many constituents are interested in individual student scores rather than in school scores.[5]

Moody cited some of the lessons learned from Maryland's experience with the MSPAP. He finds that the most valuable lesson of the last 10 years

---

[3]A criterion-referenced test is used to ascertain an individual's status with respect to a defined assessment domain.

[4]The items and tasks on the test appear to be reasonable representations of the content and skills the test is intended to measure.

[5]Since the workshop, Nancy Grasmick, Maryland's State Superintendent of Schools, has decided to replace the MSPAP with a test that is more aligned with a new high school proficiency exam and meets new federal requirements that state tests provide individual scores.

pertains to the four aspects of task development. He stressed that when a performance task is constructed it is crucial to consider these questions: (1) What is the content of the task? (2) How is the task going to be scored? (3) What materials does a task require? and (4) Can the task be administered? Moody and his colleagues have learned that a lot of good ideas cannot be administered, and a lot of tasks that can be administered are not very interesting. He recommended multiple levels of review for the tasks at different levels of the school system. Finally, he suggested the formation of an advisory group of experts to offer guidance on psychometric rigor and administration of the assessment.

ALTERNATIVE REPORTING MODELS TO THE NATIONAL REPORTING SYSTEM

Given the differences in ABE instruction and student goals across states, many presenters shared their concerns that a set of uniform, standardized performance assessments may not work within the NRS. Even though participants understood that the charge of the committee was to address the use of performance assessments within the NRS framework, a number of workshop speakers stimulated long-range thinking by describing some alternative reporting models.

Jim Impara described a model used in Nebraska at the K-12 level. The state has adopted content standards, and local school districts must report on the percentage of students who meet these standards. The school districts are allowed to choose their own assessments, but an independent group formed by the state evaluates each local assessment system using a scale of quality measures. The state uses six criteria to evaluate the assessment system of individual school districts: (1) The assessments reflect state or local standards; (2) Students have an opportunity to learn the content; (3) The assessments are free from bias or offensive situations; (4) The level is appropriate for students; (5) There is consistency in scoring; and (6) Mastery levels are appropriate. (For more information, see http://www.nde.state.ne.us [April 29, 2002].)

The state then publishes the district-reported percentage of students meeting the standards and the evaluative rating of the quality of the local assessments. Districts that receive low ratings for their assessments, but report that their students seem to be doing well, do not have as much credibility as districts with assessments that receive high ratings. The Nebraska model could be applied within the NRS in the following way: A national audit of the assessment system used by each state could be conducted, and a "weight" or grade could then be assigned to each state's system. Adjustments could be made to account for any major differences across the states.

Another model was proposed by Richard Hill and is described here even though it does not adhere to the pretest/posttest assessment design of the NRS. Hill suggested allowing ABE programs within each state to establish individual "contracts" with each student. The accountability index would be based on the proportion of individual contracts in which students met their goals. Hill believes that an advantage of this system is that it would be comparable for all types of adult education programs. For example, the same questions could be asked of all programs and all students, whether a program was designed to provide training for a specific job-related task or to provide preparation for postsecondary education.

6

Challenges in Adult Education

The discussion during the workshop highlighted a number of key challenges that must be addressed when performance assessments are used for accountability in the federal adult education system: (1) defining the domain of knowledge, skills, and abilities in a field where there is no single definition of the domain; (2) using performance assessments for multiple purposes and different audiences; (3) having the fiscal resources required for assessment development, training, implementation, and maintenance when the federal and state monies under the Workforce Investment Act (WIA) of 1998 are limited for such activities; (4) having sufficient time for assessment and learning opportunities given the structure of adult education programs and students' limited participation; and (5) developing the expertise needed for assessment development, implementation, and maintenance. This chapter discusses these challenges and their implications for alternatives identified by workshop presenters.

DEFINING A COMMON DOMAIN OF KNOWLEDGE, SKILLS, AND ABILITIES

Varied Frameworks

One very critical stage in the development of performance assessments is defining the domain of knowledge, skills, and abilities that students will be expected to demonstrate. In her remarks, Mari Pearlman said that in order to have reliable and valid assessments to compare students' outcomes across classes, programs, and states, a common domain must be used as the basis for the assessment. This poses a challenge to the field of adult education because, as several speakers pointed out, there is no consensus on the content to be assessed. As Ron Pugsley, Office of Vocational and Adult Education of the Department of Education (DOEd), reminded participants, Title II of the WIA specifies the core measures that states must use in reporting student progress (see Table 2-1), but the content underlying these measures is not operationally defined in the same way by the states and sometimes not even by all the programs within a state. In many testing programs, there is a document (called a framework) that provides a detailed outline of the content and skills to be assessed. But on the national level, no such document exists for adult education, and few states have defined the universe of content for their adult basic education programs. Hence, the extent to which specific literacy and numeracy skills are taught in a program can vary greatly depending on the characteristics of the student population and available staff.

To address this variation in instructional content, the National Institute for Literacy (NIFL) began the Equipped for the Future (EFF) initiative in 1993. Sondra Stein explained that NIFL used the results of its survey of 1,500 adults to identify the themes of family, community, work, and lifelong learning as the main purposes for which adults enroll in adult basic education programs (see Figure 6-1 for the EFF standards). NIFL then specified content standards for each theme and is now in the process of developing performance assessments aligned with the content standards. Some states (Maine, Ohio, Oregon, Tennessee, and Washington) have adopted the EFF framework and are working with NIFL in the assessment development process, while others are in the process of developing their own assessments. Although EFF represents an important movement toward common content for adult basic education programs, not all states have adopted its framework at this time.

Comparability of Performance Assessments

As discussed in Chapter 5, workshop presenters described two approaches for identifying performance assessment tasks: the critical indicator approach and the domain sampling approach. Both approaches require delineation of the domain. In order for results from one version of the assessment to be comparable to results from another version, there needs to

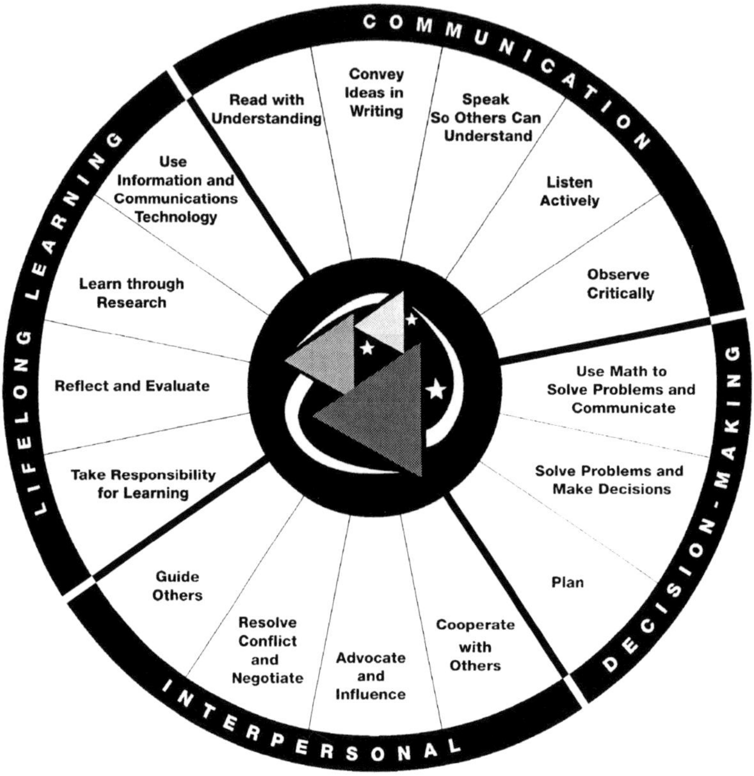

FIGURE 6-1 EFF Standards for Adult Literacy and Lifelong Learning
SOURCE: NIFL, 2002.

be a common domain with agreed-upon critical skills and knowledge and types of tasks that allow students to demonstrate these skills and knowledge. While these two approaches may be feasible on a limited level, such as in a program or within a state, it will be much more difficult to apply them across states or nationally.

USING PERFORMANCE ASSESSMENTS FOR MULTIPLE PURPOSES

Throughout the workshop, participants enumerated the varied uses for assessments in adult basic education: for diagnostic purposes, to meet accountability requirements, to provide feedback to students and/or teachers, and for program evaluation. As Pamela Moss explained, different purposes bring different kinds of validity issues, and David Thissen, Stephen Dunbar, and Jim Impara noted that it is difficult, if not impossible to develop one assessment that adequately serves such varied purposes. However, several speakers talked about ways performance assessments might be developed to serve the purpose of the NRS (National Reporting System). As suggested by Mark Reckase, Mari Pearlman, and others, the structured portfolio has the potential of serving the dual purposes of meeting accountability requirements and providing feedback to students. But for it to do so, the menu of content and tasks must be broad enough to meet the accountability requirements for the domain and to have enough examples to provide meaningful feedback to students.

Computer-based assessment could also serve the two purposes, and it has the advantage of providing rapid feedback to the student. According to Bob Bickerton and Donna Miller-Parker, use of computer-based assessment in adult basic education has been limited because of accessibility issues, costs, and training of staff. Henry Braun cautioned that it would be important to determine the types of learners for whom this modality would be appropriate before initiating its use for accountability purposes.

One factor that will need to be considered when performance assessments are used for accountability is the process of calibrating the performance assessments to the scale used for the NRS. Wendy Yen and Braun emphasized that a true calibration requires that the assessments be based on the same domains. While the developers of the tests with benchmark scores specified in the NRS attempted to calibrate their tests to the levels in ABE or ESL (depending on the test), various workshop presenters said that the calibration process was not technically accurate. Yen observed that these tests "have different content and have been developed under different criteria." She said that these conditions are not sufficient for the more stringent linking procedures such as equating or calibration. These linking procedures require equivalence of test content and examination of item and test statistics, among other things. Yen also noted that several National Research Council (NRC) reports, such as *Uncommon Measures: Equivalence and Linkage Among Educational Tests* (1999c) and *Embedding Questions: The Pursuit of a Common Measure in Uncommon Tests* (1999a), have addressed the issue of linking results from different assessments. She observed that linking issues will need to be addressed when performance assessments are used to measure students' movement on the NRS levels. She cautioned that in order for multiple performance assessments to be developed and calibrated to the NRS, they would need to measure the same domains. If they do not, then the less rigorous process of social moderation could be used to ascertain the match between scores on the assessments and the NRS levels. However, several workshop participants questioned whether social moderation was sufficiently rigorous for use in a high-stakes environment.

HAVING THE REQUIRED FISCAL RESOURCES

Assessment Development and Staff Training

As described in Chapter 2, states have limited funding to spend on assessment development, staff training, implementation, and maintenance. Several presenters emphasized both the importance of having adequate development and training processes to support the creation of quality performance assessments, and the substantial cost of these activities. In his presentation, Reckase estimated that the cost for development of a performance assessment system could total $1.5 to $2 million.

Some of the expenses are one-time costs and some recur with each administration. One-time costs are those associated with initial implementation of the assessment. Recurring costs are the expenses for ongoing item or task development, administering the test, and scoring examinees' responses. As mentioned earlier in this report, the cost for scoring responses to performance assessments or constructed-response questions is substantially higher than that for scoring selected-response questions. In addition, costs for the development of these assessments can be higher. Tasks used on performance assessments are easily memorized and, unlike selected-response items, often cannot be reused. Administration costs can also be hefty, given the time, materials, and resources required to administer performance assessments.

Eduardo Cascallar estimated that a performance assessment of language ability that he developed cost $120 per administration. Judy Alamprese noted that the current cost for an external degree program is approximately $2,000 per student, and Mark Moody stated that it is approximately $60 per student (for 180,000 students) for Maryland's MSPAP, and this amount doesn't cover the cost of test administration. States' Leadership funding under WIA, which has ranged from $100,000 to $7.5 million per state per year (with most states at the lower end of this range), provides the money states use for development and training activities. Because the federal allotment is the sole funding for these activities for most states, it is unlikely that individual states can afford substantial costs for implementing a performance assessment program. In light of this, workshop presenters suggested other options, such as the formation of consortia in which states work together or in conjunction with publishers to develop and score performance assessments. These ideas are further discussed in Chapter 7. However, the challenge to fiscal resources also extends to the administration of these assessments, especially when the national average expenditure per student in adult education programs is $374, and the 10 states with the lowest expenditures averaged only $156 per student (program year 1999).

Assessment Implementation and Maintenance

The creation of performance assessments, including specifying content domains and developing scoring rubrics as well as providing staff training, is only a portion of the cost of using these assessments. Implementing a performance assessment system and maintaining and refurbishing assessments are ongoing costs that programs must take into consideration. John Comings estimated that adult education programs could afford to spend only about $50 per student for assessment; this is inadequate for implementing a performance assessment system, according to Richard Hill, Impara, Reckase, and other speakers, given the experience of the National External Diploma Program in adult education or the K-12 system. While the presenters pointed out that there were cost differences in using the various alternative approaches to performance assessment that were suggested, none of the other assessments would cost as little as $50 per student.

Cascallar and other speakers observed that, in addition to implementation costs, there are costs associated with updating and revisions, particularly if the assessment is to meet the desire of many program staffs to have assessments that are dynamic. These updates include new development to keep the assessment current, refining scoring rubrics (particularly in the use of structured portfolios), and updating training manuals. The costs for these activities would need to be subsidized by the states or budgeted as part of the ABE programs' operational costs. In addition, there are costs associated with training staff to administer performance assessments and providing the necessary materials and other resources. A final but important cost is associated with external review of the assessments and the system. Under the Elementary and Secondary Education Act, the federal government has taken the lead in the evaluation of K-12 assessment systems. (Massachusetts is one of many states that also hire external reviewers.) Kit Viator emphasized the value of external review, commenting that it is important to let others have access to materials and come to their own independent conclusions about the strengths and weaknesses of the program.

HAVING SUFFICIENT TIME FOR ASSESSMENT AND LEARNING OPPORTUNITIES

Time is one aspect of the adult basic education service delivery system that poses significant challenges for the use of performance assessment. Time is a limited commodity for most adult education students. As mentioned in the overview and by a number of presenters, adult education students spend a limited amount of time in instruction, and they have limited time for carrying out performance assessments. Speakers queried whether this amount of time provided a sufficient "opportunity to learn." If the instructional time is not sufficient for learning, then the assessment may not be a reliable test of students' educational progress. The speakers noted that student persistence in regularly attending classes and completing a course of study is a critical factor for most adult education programs. Lack of student persistence appears to be a characteristic of the system that is unaffected by attempts to remedy it.

In suggesting alternative ways to construct performance assessments, Reckase described the challenge of addressing the "information channel" in which the goal is to assess as much skill and knowledge as possible within a specified amount of time. As stated earlier, Reckase estimated that 50 to 100 selected-response items can be administered to an adult in an hour, while no more than 10 performance assessments can be given in the same period of time. With the current levels of student persistence, students' patterns of participation in adult basic education, and the limited number of hours that some programs operate, the amount of time required for adminstration is a critical factor to consider when state and local administrators are determining the feasibility of using performance assessment.

DEVELOPING EXPERTISE

A refrain heard throughout the workshop was the need to have trained and qualified individuals for all phases of performance assessment development, administration, and scoring. A number of presenters observed that the technical expertise of most adult basic education program staff is not sufficient for them to undertake assessment development. Assessment development is a technical field with stringent guidelines, and several presenters suggested that states and programs work collaboratively with psychometricians in the assessment development process. One possible role for adult education staff in the development process might be to provide the applications of content that can be used in the development of assessment tasks.

Another strategy might be to use assessment approaches that minimize the requirement for trained staff to administer and score the assessments, such as computer-based assessment. When both the administration and the scoring can be done electronically, staff do not have to perform these functions. If program staff are to be responsible for assessment administration and scoring, then experts are needed to provide professional development on a periodic basis. All of the activities involved in developing, administering, and scoring performance assessment systems require not only expertise but also time and fiscal resources.

7

Options and Strategies

This section of the report summarizes the various suggestions for practical steps that could be taken in making performance assessments in adult education useful to educators and students, psychometrically acceptable, adequate for national reporting purposes, and feasible without overtaxing the personnel or fiscal resources of any state or program. The strategies presented are grouped under the problem they are meant to address.

PROBLEM 1: LIMITED RESOURCES FOR THE DEVELOPMENT OF ASSESSMENTS

A common refrain from workshop participants was that considerable resources are required to create, pilot test, score, and norm assessments of any sort, as well as develop guidelines for interpreting their results. Developing good assessments is time-consuming and expensive, and it also demands specific expertise that is somewhat rare and may be difficult to access. Thus, it would be inefficient for each program or even each state to develop its own assessments, even if the resources were available to do so. Furthermore, in the current funding situation, many smaller states and states with particularly limited resources for adult education are simply unable to assume the task of developing assessments on their own. Workshop participants offered a variety of strategies to address the resource issue.

Pooling Resources Through Consortia

One strategy for overcoming the problems posed by limited resources is to form consortia. Yen, Braun, Plake, and Impara suggested that states form consortia in which they could pool their resources to find the expertise needed and to do the work required to develop assessments useful to all of them. In forming consortia, states would have to team up with others that have defined the content to be assessed in similar ways. The states within a consortium would also need to have adult education programs with a similar profile (in the percent of English-language learners or the distribution of GED versus employment preparation students, for example) and thus with similar demands on the assessments. As Barbara Plake said, "When you have limited resources and a common set of regulations, it makes great sense ... to circle the wagons and maximize the utility of the resources you have in developing these programs." The work of the National Institute for Literacy with Equipped for the Future (EFF) could also produce benefits similar to those of a consortium as there is a defined domain and predetermined assessments.

Utilizing Test Publishers' Resources

Another strategy is to utilize the resources available through test publishers. Involving test publishers in this work has a number of potential advantages. The test publishers can access the expertise needed for test development; they have fiscal resources to invest in test development; and they stand to gain from well-designed tests because they are in a position to market and profit from them. Several speakers suggested establishing agreements with publishers to develop assessments for particular purposes that can be used by many states or state consortia and can also be marketed more widely. This would be an effective way to reduce demands on state resources while developing usable assessments. Wendy Yen recommended that directors of adult education programs seek guidance from state testing directors in the K-12 sector because they are greatly skilled in working with publishers to develop the kinds of tests they want.

Collaborating with Psychometricians

Workshop speakers encouraged consultation with psychometricians. Psychometric professionals have undergone highly specialized training in designing and implementing assessment programs. Workshop presenters such as Ronald Hambleton, Stephen Sireci, and other psychometricians expressed their willingness to become involved in the challenges currently facing adult basic education. Indeed, one of the nice messages of the workshop was the enthusiasm and interest with which the psychometricians in attendance addressed the issues formulated by the adult education specialists. One suggestion that arose from workshop discussion was that the federal government establish a panel of expert psychometricians to provide guidance to the Department of Education (DOEd) on issues related to the National Reporting System (NRS) and other measurement concerns.

Prioritizing Assessment Goals

A final strategy discussed was ways to prioritize assessment goals so as to make the test development tasks more manageable. Several presenters recommended narrowing the domain coverage assessed as one means to accomplish this. Not all aspects of student growth or program functioning need to be extensively assessed or assessed with shared instruments. The demands of test development could be greatly reduced by being practical and focused in thinking about what needs to be assessed for the purposes of program and/or state comparisons.

PROBLEM 2: DEVELOPING A USABLE SUITE OF ASSESSMENTS

A common refrain throughout the workshop was that a single assessment, no matter how perfect, will never serve all needs. One suggestion aimed at improving the assessment landscape within adult education was to think about a serviceable "suite" of assessments, that is, having a variety or array of tests, including multiple-choice tests and various kinds of performance assessments tasks, available for use by adult educators. These tests could be used for particular purposes including instruction, local benchmarking, within-state program evaluation, and national reporting. They could be adapted to the needs of the various groups served by adult basic education programs, including GED students, adults with literacy problems related to learning disabilities, adult ESL learners with and without educational experience and literacy skills in their first languages, and so on. Workshop participants seemed to agree that assessments that are divorced in content from the goals of instruction are not useful for the student or the teacher; in the ABE system, as within the K-12 system, alignment of standards, curriculum, and assessment is key. Kit Viator pointed out that the state of Massachusetts placed a great deal of emphasis on the alignment of both content and performance standards with assessments. Leah Bricker discussed the work of Project 2061 of the American Association for the Advancement of Science (AAAS) on developing an analysis procedure for the alignment of K-12 math and science assessments with national and state standards. AAAS's procedure reveals the degree of alignment between a state's standards and its assessments; this is helpful for states that are evaluating the alignment of assessment tasks to specific learning goals. Achieving alignment requires formulating standards (much harder in ABE than in K-12) and including measures of curricular content, as well as selecting or generating appropriate assessments.

One aspect of the ABE programs that must be considered in the context of an array of assessments is that students often come to their programs without a specific goal or credential in mind. In making suggestions about the components of a suite of assessments, workshop participants noted the importance of strategies for using technology, making decisions about when to use which assessments, and improving practitioners' and administrators' knowledge base about the values and limitations of assessment. They also noted the trade-offs associated with developing and using performance assessments. First, like all kinds of assessments, the development of performance assessments requires a clear definition of curricular goals and content. Second, performance assessments are expensive and technically difficult to develop; the current system may be too restricted by limited funding, time, and expertise to develop high-quality performance assessments. Third, good performance assessments take a lot of time, which must be subtracted from instructional time (which is quite limited in ABE). If the instructors do not see the connection between assessments and instruction, they can undermine validity in their presentation of the assessment exercise to the student. Moreover, many students are mandated by the court or social services office to attend a program; others come voluntarily, but do not seek any particular credential; this makes it hard to define what outcomes can be judged as "good enough." If students perceive there is little at stake for them, they may be unmotivated to perform their best, and this, too, can undermine validity.

A number of workshop participants stressed that good assessment systems are dynamic. They should be expected to change over time in order to remain current. Their development is never finished because the perfect test has never been written. When tests are used for purposes of accountability and of supporting instruction, assessment items should be shared with the public at regular intervals. This is done regularly at the K-12 level, as both Viator and Mark Moody noted. Public release of items means development must be ongoing. Thus, assessments—the items used, the scoring, the guidelines for administration, and so on—need to be reconstituted regularly to incorporate lessons learned from previous administrations.

Making Use of Available Technology

On the one hand, developing computer-administered tests can be extremely expensive and requires specialized expertise; on the other hand, these tests can greatly decrease the testing burden by providing brief, efficient, individually adapted versions of tests, and they can increase the value of test data by ensuring accurate calculation of students' proficiency levels. Plake suggested that computer delivery has the advantages of on-demand administration and immediate scoring to provide preliminary test results at the conclusion of the testing session, and it can achieve higher precision of measurement with fewer items and potentially less administration time. Although much assessment in adult education will continue to take place without the use of technology, Cascallar, Braun, Impara, and others strongly urged the strategic use of technology for certain limited purposes. Sireci said that computer-based testing (CBT) could minimize testing time and be widely accessible to students in remote locations. He recommended reviewing how the Test of English as a Foreign Language (TOEFL) and ACCUPLACER are able to administer their tests in a cost-efficient manner.[1] Hambleton noted that CBT could be useful in developing shorter and more precise assessments targeted to ability and in improving the ease of scoring and testing security. Finally, Henry Braun endorsed the idea of using technology as a vehicle for delivering professional development. He offered the following advice:

> A professional development program that combines a couple of hours of contract time with rich materials on the Web may be a way of circumventing some of these issues for the teachers. If you create a higher level of expertise

---

[1]For the Test of English as a Foreign Language (TOEFL), see www.toefl.org. [May 14, 2002]. For ACCUPLACER, see www.collegeboard.com/accuplacer/html/accupla1.html. [May 14, 2002].

among teachers, the investment pays off enormously in terms of their influence on the students.

Using Test Development to Create Professional Development

At the workshop, concerns were voiced about the demands of the NRS in adult education and the increased demands for accountability in education in general. These concerns derive in part from the fear that tests used for comparability judgments will supplant tests that practitioners know to be useful in their own instruction. Enhancing teachers' understanding of the variety of assessments that are available, the various purposes for which they should be used, and their specific demands could help practitioners use the full variety of assessments in a more targeted way. Limited resources and an enormous need to improve instruction are likely to remain constant characteristics of the ABE system. Under these circumstances, Sireci suggested utilizing the NRS procedure as a mechanism for supporting instructional enhancement and as an opportunity for professional development. He commented that work with K-12 teachers in item-writing workshops, standard-setting studies, and content validity studies has been informative and useful in developing better tests and in improving teachers' instructional practice. Too few states are offering professional development on developing assessments, reviewing student performance in a guided way, formulating standards for acceptable performance, and scoring assessments.

As noted in the overview of the adult education system in Chapter 2, many classrooms are served by instructors who lack training or expertise for their major task of teaching, let alone for implementing and using assessments. Speakers raised concerns that a focus on developing assessment strategies without concomitant attention to instruction would constitute a misdirection of resources. Hambleton stressed the need for training adult education teachers in topics such as constructing and scoring a test and interpreting data to ensure that tests are used appropriately in the classroom and that test results are understood by the educators.

Using Performance Assessments Appropriately

In many situations, teachers and students appear to value performance assessments over other sorts of assessments. Performance assessments have face validity and a sense of authenticity, and they are thought to have considerable educational value because of their capacity to reflect a wide variety of accomplishments and to be connected organically to the material taught. However, data from performance assessments are also time-consuming to collect and to analyze, and they provide less direct comparability between students, programs, and states than other forms of assessment. Thus, many speakers at the workshop suggested that performance assessments be used selectively and in combination with a variety of other assessment instruments, including standardized multiple-choice tests.

Several speakers endorsed the use of a mix of performance and traditional assessments for instructional purposes in the classroom. It was suggested that optimal use of assessments would be ensured if programs and educators were given a strategy for selecting the right combination of assessments that would match the time and money available and provide the information needed.

Cultivating Existing Knowledge About Performance Assessment

Discussions at the workshop called attention to the fact that performance assessments can benefit from the contributions of committed amateurs, but they cannot achieve sufficient levels of validity, reliability, and comparability without the substantial involvement of a professional psychometrician. Chapters 3 and 5 outlined clear procedures for creating performance assessments. Knowledge of the assessment process and the *Standards for Educational and Psychological Testing* (American Educational Research Association et al., 1999), little of which seems to be currently available within the adult education community, would help states and local programs make educated decisions about implementing performance assessments and would provide valuable guidance during the development process.

Developing Program Support for Alternative Assessments

Well-designed and well-maintained portfolios are one component of a suite of assessments useful for instructional purposes that could also be used as input to a summative assessment of student progress. Plake stressed the potential of portfolios for fulfilling the reporting needs of the states, while at the same time providing useful information about students' progress. However, she cautioned that cost, time, and resources are concerns. Furthermore, the reliability of portfolios as a single basis for student assessment has been challenged in the K-8 educational system (Koretz,

1994). Additionally, if instructors are devoting time and energy to the compilation of portfolios, some attention to the question of their optimal use for a variety of purposes is clearly warranted. Plake and several others suggested that using portfolios as part of a larger suite of assessments is an idea that deserves further exploration.

PROBLEM 3: DATA QUALITY

Thus far the primary focus of this report has been on quality standards for performance assessments. In addition, there are issues of quality in maintaining records of students' performance and other data required by the NRS. Local programs collect the initial data on students and forward data to the states. States are required to implement and maintain a computerized student-level data system and to forward valid and reliable information to the DOEd. At each data collection point, quality controls need to be in place to ensure that data represent what they are intended to represent and that they can be interpreted in the desired ways. The meaning of the collected data relies on the diligence and accuracy of recordkeeping by all parties.

The data the DOEd receives from the states are used to obtain national totals and averages for the various indicators required by the NRS. These averages are used by states as they negotiate their levels of performance, and they are reported to Congress and other interested parties. Data from individual states are used to assess whether they have met their negotiated levels of performance and, thereby, meet the WIA Title II component to qualify for an incentive grant.

An accountability system like the NRS is inherently dependent on the quality and integrity of the data it accepts. However, the NRS does not yet provide minimum standards for data quality or for auditing or other verification of the integrity of the data collected. Further, it is not clear that states and local programs have the resources and systems in place to collect and maintain the mandated data. For instance, Bob Bickerton presented results from a survey conducted in the first half of the current performance period (program year 2001): In their responses to the survey, 18 states reported that they had not yet implemented the required systems.

Issues of data quality enter into the validity of analyses conducted with the data. Bickerton provided examples of the improbable situations that can emerge when standards for data are not yet implemented. In one report, a state with an average of 116 hours of student attendance per year indicated that 36 percent of the students completed a federally defined instructional level (i.e., progressed from one educational functioning level to the next). Another state with only 31 hours per student per year reported that almost 68 percent of the students completed a federal level in program year 2000. In a second example, a state that spent $2,084 per student per year reported that 36.7 percent of the students completed a federal level in program year 1999. Another state that spent only $233 per student per year reported that 90.2 percent of the students completed a federal level in program year 1999. While there is a chance that these results are true, they may also reflect inaccuracies or inconsistencies in the way data are collected, maintained, and reported. If the goal is to achieve comparability across states, quality controls need to be in place to ensure that the meaning of data is consistent.

PROBLEM 4: ACHIEVING A BASIS FOR COMPARABILITY USING PERFORMANCE ASSESSMENTS

States that decide to implement performance assessments will need multiple versions of the assessment. To avoid practice effects, different versions will be needed for pretests and posttests. For security reasons, different versions will be needed for different testing years. Furthermore, because states will develop their own performance assessments, there will be different versions from state to state. A major problem with performance assessments is the difficulty of achieving comparability across different versions of the assessments. One goal of the NRS is to make comparisons—comparisons of students' performance from pretest to posttest and comparisons from state to state. For instance, the goal is that student performance that is interpreted as moving to the next level in Oregon would also qualify a student to move to the next level in Ohio. This requires a common basis for comparing performance.

Workshop participants voiced concern that performance assessments may not generate adequate levels of comparability. Some thought it might be possible to implement a systematic process that used social moderation to roughly align scores from a variety of performances. Widely used tests such as the TABE, CASAS, and others could also be used as part of the process to establish a link between performance assessments and NRS levels. Under social moderation, judgment is used to align scores on assessments with one another or with a common reporting scale even though the assessments may measure somewhat different knowledge with different kinds of tasks (Linn, 1993; Mislevy, 1992). The question remains whether this level of comparability would be sufficient in the high-stakes environment established by the ABE National Reporting System. The crux of the issue is the degree to which students placed at one level of the NRS with one assessment would be placed at a different level with another assessment—a source of uncertainty in addition to other measurement error associated with scores on either of the two assessments (e.g., due to low reliability levels).

There are ways to estimate the uncertainty associated with using social moderation. One way would be to have multiple panels of experts independently carry out the alignment task and then estimate the frequencies of classification discrepancies that would result (that is, the frequency with which the judgments varied from one panel to the next). It should also be noted that the real impact of the social-moderation uncertainty depends on the way test results are used. For instance, one proposed use of test results under the NRS is to compare performance across states. Here, differences in the way scores are aligned will influence estimates of the proportions of students in each state who are considered to be performing at the various NRS levels. Increases or decreases in the proportion of a state's students at a given level could simply be due to differences in the way the scores are aligned (e.g. variability in the judgment-based decisions). More lenient judgments (i.e., lower cut scores associated with an NRS level) could increase the proportions; harsher judgments (i.e., higher cut scores associated with the NRS level) could decrease the proportions. Another proposed use of results, however, is to set gain-score targets independently within states. This use is affected much less by the uncertainty associated with social moderation, as it only concerns changes on a single assessment (i.e., the state's own assessment), even though the scores may have been mapped through moderation onto a common NRS metric.

Develop Benchmarks Identified with NRS Levels

A major challenge to the use of performance assessments for accountability purposes, such as those stated in the NRS, is that performance assessments usually cannot be designed to be precise enough to reflect relatively small developmental increments in skill. Because of external factors in their lives, a large majority of ABE students participate in education programs for a limited length of time and study with limited intensity. Hence, it is not likely that their progress will show up as movement from one NRS level to the next. Several speakers expressed concern that students might not actually show increments in skill sufficient to be measured by performance assessments. Some also recommended that midway points be identified within a NRS level to address this issue.

Several concerns were also highlighted about using NRS levels to measure student proficiency and educational gain, regardless of which assessment is administered (see Chapter 4 for further discussion of this issue). Several speakers suggested engaging in a consensual effort to develop benchmarks identified with the transitions between NRS levels and possibly even with identified midway points. This could generate a basis for decisions about student progress within the context of the NRS design without undermining the current use of the wide variety of assessments in ABE programs across the country.

Balancing Comparability with Flexibility

The issues related to comparability of the assessments and the methods of establishing linking or cross-walking of assessments have been highlighted throughout this report. Several speakers called for work on linking paper-and-pencil as well as performance assessments. Braun and others recommended that the process of matching NRS descriptive levels with benchmarks (or cut-scores) by a variety of test publishers be revisited to be assured that it can support the inferences about students' skill level. No one at the workshop thought that a simple basis for linkage across the various assessments would emerge, but possibilities exist for developing post hoc subtests within those tests that might aid in linking, using social moderation or statistical moderation (e.g., EFF benchmarking tasks), or might help in defining ranges of scores on the various tests that could be considered roughly equivalent to one another.

Greater comparability could be achieved through standardization (i.e., same content standards and tests across states), but it would come at the cost of decreased flexibility at the program or state level in choice of assessments. Thus the trade-offs need to be kept in mind. In the words of Braun:

> We gain evidential value and construct representation but we pay a cost . . . in terms of development, scoring, testing time, and reliability . . . How they play off against each other will have to be worked out in the context of our particular purposes and constraints.

References

ACCUPLACER. (2002). Available: <http://www.collegeboard.com/accuplacer/html/accupla1.html>. [May 14, 2002].

American Educational Research Association, American Psychological Association, and National Council on Measurement in Education. (1999). *Standards for educational and psychological testing.* Washington, DC: Author.

Ananda, S. (2000). *Equipped for the Future assessment report: How instructors can support adult learners through performance-based assessment* (EX 0110P). Washington, DC: U.S. Department of Education.

Anastasi, A. (1988). *Psychological testing.* New York: Macmillan.

Bachman, L.F. (1990). *Fundamental considerations in language testing.* Oxford: Oxford University Press.

Bachman, L.F. and Palmer, A.S. (1996). *Language testing in practice.* Oxford: Oxford University Press.

Bond, L. (1995). Unintended consequences of performance assessment: Issues of bias and fairness. *Educational Measurement: Issues and Practices, 14*(4), 21-24.

Brennan, R.L. (1983). *Elements of generalizability theory.* Iowa City, IA: ACT Publications.

Brennan, R.L. (2001). An essay on the history and future of reliability from the perspective of replications. *Journal of Educational Measurement, 38*(4), 295-317.

Brennan, R.L., and Johnson, E.G. (1995). Generalizability of performance assessments. *Educational Measurement: Issues and Practices, 14*(4), 9-12.

Camilli, G., and Shepard, L.A. (1994). *Methods for identifying biased test items.* Thousand Oaks, CA: Sage.

Cole, N.S., and Moss, P.M. (1993). Bias in test use. In R.L. Linn (Ed.), *Educational Measurement* (3rd ed.). Phoenix, AZ: Oryx.

Comings, J., Sum, A., and Uvin, J. (2000). *New skills for a new economy: Adult education's key role in sustaining economic growth and expanding opportunity.* Boston: Massachusetts Institute for a New Commonwealth.

Comrey, A.L., and Lee, H.B. (1992). *A first course in factor analysis* (2nd ed.). Hillsdale, NJ: Erlbaum.

Crocker, L., and Algina, J. (1986). *Introduction to classical and modern test theory.* Orlando, FL: Harcourt Brace Jovanovich.

Cureton, E.E., and D'Agostino, R.B. (1983). *Factor analysis: An applied approach.* Hillsdale, NJ: Erlbaum.

Dunbar, S., Koretz, D., and Hoover, H.D. (1991). Quality control in the use of performance assessment. *Applied Measurement in Education, 4*(4), 289-303.

Feldt, L.S., and Brennan, R.L. (1993). Reliability. In R.L. Linn (Ed.), *Educational Measurement* (3rd ed.). Phoenix, AZ: Oryx.

Gorsuch, R.L. (1983). *Factor analysis.* Hillsdale, NJ: Erlbaum.

Green, B.F. (1995). Comparability of scores from performance assessments. *Educational Measurement: Issues and Practices, 14*(4), 13-15.

Hambleton, R.K., Swaminathan, H., and Rogers, H.J. (1991). *Fundamentals of item response theory.* Newbury Park, CA: Sage.

Harris, C.W. (Ed.). (1963). *Problems in measuring change.* Madison, WI: University of Wisconsin Press.

Holland, P.W., and Wainer, H. (1993). *Differential item functioning.* Newbury Park, NJ: Erlbaum.

Kaufman, P., Kwon, J.Y., Klein, S., and Chapman, C.D. (2000). *Dropout rates in the United States: 1999* (NCES 2001-22). Washington, DC: U.S. Department of Education, National Center for Education Statistics.

Kolen, M.J., and Brennan, R.L. (1995). *Testing equating methods and practices.* New York: Springer.

Koretz, D. (1994). *The evolution of a portfolio program: The impact and quality of the Vermont Portfolio Program in its second year (1992-93)* (ERIC #ED379301). Los Angeles: National Center for Research and Evaluation, Standards, and Student Testing.

Koretz, D., Stetcher, B., Klein, S., and McCaffrey, D. (1994). The Vermont Portfolio Assessment Program: Findings and implications. *Educational Measurement: Issues and Practice, 13*(3), 5-16.

Kunnan, A.J. (Ed.) (2000). *Fairness and validation in language assessment.* Cambridge: Cambridge University Press.

LeMahieu, P.G., Gitomer, D.H., and Eresh, J.T. (1995). Portfolios in large-scale assessments: Difficult but not impossible. *Educational Measurement: Issues and Practice, 14*(3), 11-16, 25-28.

Linn, R.L. (1993). Linking results of distinct assessments. *Applied Measurement in Education, 6*(1), 83-102.

Linn, R.L., Gronlund, N.E., and Davis, K.M. (1999). *Measurement and assessment in teaching* (8th ed.). Upper Saddle River, NJ: Prentice-Hall.

Messick, S. (1989). Validity. In R.L. Linn (Ed.), *Educational Measurement* (3rd ed.). New York: Macmillan.

Messick, S. (1995). Standards of validity and the validity of standards in performance assessment. *Educational Measurement: Issues and Practices, 14*(4), 5-8.

Microsoft Certification Program. (2002). Available: <http://www.Microsoft.com/traincert/mcp>. [March 28, 2002].

Millman, J., and Greene, J. (1993). The specification and development of tests of achievement and ability. In R.L. Linn (Ed.), *Educational Measurement* (3rd ed.). Phoenix, AZ: Oryx.

Mislevy, R.J. (1992). *Linking educational assessments: Concepts, issues, methods and prospects* (ERIC #ED353302). Princeton, NJ: Educational Testing Service.

Mislevy, R.J. (1995). *Linking adult literacy assessments.* Princeton, NJ: Educational Testing Service.

National Board for Professional Teaching Standards. (2000). *A distinction that matters: Why national teacher certification makes sense.* Arlington, VA: Author.

National Council of Teachers of Mathematics. (2000). *Principles and standards for school mathematics.* Reston, VA: Author.

National Institute for Literacy. (2002). *EFF standards for adult literacy and lifelong learning.* Available: <http://www.nifl.gov/lincs/collections/eff/eff_standards.html>. [May 1, 2002].

National Reporting System. (2002). *6 levels of ABE or ESL.* Available: <http://www.oei-tech.com/nrs/>. [April 29, 2002].

National Research Council. (1997). *Educating one and all: Students with disabilities and standards-based reform.* Committee on Goals 2000 and the Inclusion of Students with Disabilities, L.M. McDonnell, M.J. McLaughlin, and P. Morison (Eds.). Commission on Behavioral and Social Sciences and Education. Washington, DC: National Academy Press.

National Research Council. (1999a). *Embedding questions: The pursuit of a common measure in uncommon tests.* Committee on Embedding Common Test Items in State and District Assessments, D.M. Koretz, M.W. Bertenthal, and B.F. Green (Eds.). Board on Testing and Assessment, Commission on Behavioral and Social Sciences and Education. Washington, DC: National Academy Press.

National Research Council. (1999b). *High stakes: Testing for tracking, promotion, and graduation.* Committee on Appropriate Test Use, J.P. Heubert and R.M. Hauser (Eds.). Commission on Behavioral and Social Sciences and Education. Washington, DC: National Academy Press.

National Research Council. (1999c). *Uncommon measures: Equivalency and linkage among educational tests.* Committee on Equivalency and Linkage of Educational Tests, M.J. Feuer, P.W. Holland, B.F. Green, M.W. Bertenthal, and F.C. Hemphill (Eds.). Board on Testing and Assessment, Commission on Behavioral and Social Sciences and Education. Washington, DC: National Academy Press.

National Research Council. (2001a). *Knowing what students know: The science and design of educational assessment.* Committee on the Foundation of Assessment, J. Pellegrino, N. Chudowsky, and R. Glaser (Eds.). Division of Behavioral and Social Sciences and Education. Washington, DC: National Academy Press.

National Research Council. (2001b). *Testing teacher candidates: The role of licensure tests in improving teacher quality.* Committee on Assessment and Teacher Quality, K.J. Mitchell, D.Z. Robinson, B.S. Plake, and K.T. Knowles (Eds.). Board on Testing and Assessment, Division of Behavioral and Social Sciences and Education. Washington, DC: National Academy Press.

Nitko, A.J. (2001). *Educational assessment of students* (3rd ed.). Upper Saddle River, NJ: Prentice-Hall.

Popham, W.J. (1999). *Classroom assessment: What teachers need to know* (2nd ed.). Boston: Allyn and Bacon.

Popham, W.J. (2000). *Modern educational measurement: Practical guidelines for educational leaders* (3rd ed.). Boston: Allyn and Bacon.

Reckase, M.D. (1995). Portfolio assessment: A theoretical estimate of score reliability. *Educational Measurement: Issues and Practice, 14*(1), 12-14.

Reckase, M.D., and Welch, C. (1999). Advances in portfolio assessment with applications to urban school populations. In M.T. Nettles and A.L. Nettles (Eds.), *Measuring up: Challenges minorities face in educational assessment.* Boston: Kluwer.

Shavelson, R.J., Baxter, G.P., and Gao, X. (1993). Sampling variability of performance assessments. *Journal of Educational Measurement, 30*(3), 215-232.

Shavelson, R., and Webb, N. (1991). *Generalizability theory: A primer.* Newbury Park, CA: Sage.

St. Pierre, R.G., Swartz, J.P., Gamse, S., Murray, S., Deck, D., and Nickel, P. (1995). *National evaluation of the Even Start Family Literacy Program: Final report.* Cambridge, MA: Abt Associates.

Test of English as a Foreign Language. (2002). Available: <http:/www.toefl.org>. [May 14, 2002].

Thissen, D. (2001). Comments on Performance Assessments for Adult Education: Exploring the Measurement Issues. Paper commissioned by the Committee on Alternatives for Assessing Adult Education and Literacy Programs. Center for Eduation. National Research Council.

Thorndike, R.L., and Hagen, E.P. (1977). *Measurement and evaluation in psychology and education* (4th ed.). New York: Wiley.

U.S. Department of Education. (2001a). *Measures and methods for the National Reporting System for Adult Education: Implementation guidelines.* Washington, DC: Author, Division of Adult Education and Literacy, Office of Vocational and Adult Education.

U.S. Department of Education. (2001b). *State-administered adult education program fiscal year 1998 expenditures (July 1, 1998-June/September 30, 2000).* Washington, DC: Author, Division of Adult Education and Literacy.

U.S. Department of Education. (2001c). *State reported hours of attendance in adult education programs (1997-2000).* Washington, DC: Author, Division of Adult Education and Literacy.

U.S. Medical Licensing Examination. (2002). Available: <http://www.uslc.org>. [May 14, 2002].

Wainer, H., Dorans, N.J., Eignor, D., Flaugher, R., Green, B.F., Mislevy, R.J., Steinberg, L., and Thissen, D. (2000). *Computerized adaptive testing: A primer* (2nd ed.). Mahwah, NJ: Erlbaum.

Workforce Investment Act of 1998 (H.R. 1385), 105th Cong., 2nd Sess. (1998).

Zumbo, B.D. (1999). The simple difference score as an inherently poor measure of change. Some reality, much mythology. In B. Thompson (Ed.), *Advances in Social Science Methodology, Volume 5* (pp. 269-304). Greenwich, CT: JAI Press.

APPENDIX A
Workshop Agenda

The National Academies
Board on Testing and Assessment (BOTA)

Performance Assessments for Adult Education:
Exploring the Measurement Issues
State Plaza Hotel
2116 F Street, NW Diplomat Room
December 12-13, 2001

December 12th

8:00 – 8:30	Continental Breakfast
8:30 – 8:45	**Welcome and Introductions** Pasquale DeVito, Director of BOTA Bob Mislevy, Chair of the Committee on Alternatives for Assessing Adult Education and Literacy Programs Member of BOTA, University of Maryland, College Park
8:45 – 9:45	PANEL 1: POLICY CONTEXT **Assessment in the Context of the Adult Education and Literacy System** John Comings, National Center for the Study of Adult Learning and Literacy, Harvard Graduate School of Education

Overview of the Workforce Investment Act and National Reporting System
Mike Dean, Office of Vocational and Adult Education, U.S. Department of Education

Equipped for the Future: A Standards-Based Approach to Defining and Measuring Results in the Adult Education and Literacy System
Sondra Stein, National Institute for Literacy, Washington, DC

Discussion Facilitator: Judy Alamprese, Abt Associates, Bethesda, MD

9:45 –10:00 Break

10:00 – 11:30 **PANEL 2: DEVELOPING PERFORMANCE ASSESSMENTS**

Using the *Standards for Educational and Psychological Testing*
Pamela Moss, University of Michigan

Developing High-Quality Performance Assessments
Stephen Dunbar, University of Iowa

Discussion Facilitator: Neal Schmitt, Michigan State University

11:30 – 12:30 Lunch

12:30 – 2:00 **PANEL 3: LESSONS LEARNED FROM OTHER CONTEXTS AND DISCIPLINES**

Lessons Learned from Implementing the External High School Diploma Program
Judy Alamprese, Abt Associates, Bethesda, MD

Lessons from K-12 State Assessments:

- **Lessons Learned from the Maryland School Performance Assessment Program (MSPAP)**
  Mark Moody, Maryland Department of Education

- **Standards-Based K-12 Testing: Lessons from the Massachusetts Comprehensive Assessment System (MCAS)**
  Kit Viator, Massachusetts Department of Education

Performance Assessment: Some Issues and Lessons from Implementation in the Field of Language Assessment
Eduardo Cascallar, American Institutes for Research, Washington, DC

2:00 – 2:15 Break

2:15 – 3:45 **PANEL 3 CONTINUED**

- **Assessing Numeracy**
  Myrna Manly, El Camino College, Torrance, CA

- **AAAS/Project 2061's Assessment Analysis Work**
  Leah Bricker, American Association for the Advancement of Science, Washington, DC

- **Phonological Awareness Literacy Screening (PALS): A Statewide, Curriculum-Embedded, Performance-Based Screening Tool with Complimentary Internet Support**
  Marcia Invernizzi and Joanne Meier, Curry School of Education, University of Virginia

Discussion Facilitator: Susan Cowles, Linn-Benton Community College, Covallis, OR

3:45 – 4:00 Break

4:00 – 5:00 **PANEL 4: DISCUSSION, SYNTHESIS, AND HIGHLIGHTING OF MAIN ISSUES**

Discussants:

- Cheryl Keenan, Pennsylvania Department of Education
- Jim Impara, Buros Institute of Assessment Consultation and Outreach, Lincoln, Nebraska
- Richard Hill, National Center for the Improvement of Educational Assessment

Discussion Facilitator: Bob Mislevy, University of Maryland, College Park

5:00 **Adjourn**

December 13th

7:45 – 8:15 Continental Breakfast

8:15 – 9:30 **PANEL 5: GUIDELINES AND STANDARDS FOR PROPERTIES OF ADULT ASSESSMENT**

Using the Results of Complex Tasks to Assess the Outcomes of Adult Education
Mark Reckase, Michigan State University

Comparability: The Search for Meaning
Henry Braun, Educational Testing Service

9:30 – 9:45 Break

9:45 – 11:00 **Performance Assessments for Adult Education: How to Design Performance Tasks**
Mari Pearlman, Educational Testing Service

Discussion Facilitator: Bob Mislevy, University of Maryland, College Park

11:00 – 11:45 **Panel 6: Implications for Applying the NRS**

From a State Perspective: Aligning Skills and Learning Gains to the NRS
Fran Tracy-Mumford, Delaware Department of Public Instruction

Implementing a Standard Assessment System—A Local Perspective
Donna Miller-Parker, Shoreline Community College, Seattle, WA

11:45 – 12:30 Lunch

12:30 – 1:45 **PANEL 6 CONTINUED**

A Test Publisher's Perspective on the NRS
Wendy Yen, K-12 Works, Educational Testing Service

How Ready Is ABE for High-Stakes Assessment?
Bob Bickerton, Massachusetts Department of Education

Discussion Facilitator: Catherine Snow, Harvard Graduate School of Education

1:45 – 2:00 Break

2:00 – 4:30 **PANEL 7: CONCLUSIONS AND SYNTHESIS**

Discussants:

- Ronald Hambleton, University of Massachusetts, Amherst
- David Thissen, University of North Carolina at Chapel Hill
- Barbara Plake, Oscar and Luella Buros Center for Testing, University of Nebraska, Lincoln
- Stephen Sireci, University of Massachusetts, Amherst

Discussion Facilitator: Lyle Bachman, University of California, Los Angeles

4:30 **Closing Comments**
Bob Mislevy, Chair of the Committee on Alternatives for Assessing Adult Education and Literacy Programs
Member of BOTA, University of Maryland, College Park

4:45 **Adjourn**

APPENDIX

B

Workshop Participants

Workshop on Performance Assessments for Adult Education:
Exploring the Measurement Issues
December 12-13, 2001

COMMITTEE ON ALTERNATIVES FOR ASSESSING ADULT EDUCATION AND LITERACY PROGRAMS

Robert J. Mislevy (*Chair*), Professor, Department of Measurement, Statistics, and Evaluation, University of Maryland at College Park
Judith A. Alamprese, Principal Associate, Abt Associates Inc.
Lyle F. Bachman, Professor and Chair, Department of Applied Linguistics and TESL, University of California at Los Angeles
Robert Bickerton, Director, Adult and Community Learning Services, Massachusetts Department of Education
John P. Comings, Senior Research Associate Lecturer on Education and Director of the National Center for the Study of Adult Learning and Literacy, Harvard Graduate School of Education
Susan K. Cowles, Instructor, Linn-Benton Community College, Corvallis, Oregon
Neal Schmitt, Professor, Department of Psychology, Michigan State University
Catherine E. Snow, Henry Lee Shattuck Professor of Education, Graduate School of Education, Harvard University

Presenters

Henry Braun, Distinguished Presidential Appointee and Managing Director of Literacy Services, Educational Testing Service

Leah A. Bricker, Senior Program Associate with Project 2061, American Association for the Advancement of Science

Eduardo Cascallar, Principal Research Scientist, American Institutes for Research

R. Michael Dean, Staff Member in the Division of Adult Education and Literacy at the Office of Vocational and Adult Education, U.S. Department of Education

Stephen B. Dunbar, Professor of Educational Measurement and Statistics, College of Education, University of Iowa

Ronald K. Hambleton, Distinguished University Professor, Center for Educational Assessment, University of Massachusetts at Amherst

Richard K. Hill, Founder and Executive Director, National Center for the Improvement of Educational Assessment, Inc.

James Impara, Director, Buros Institute of Assessment Consultation and Outreach

Marcia Invernizzi, Professor of Reading, Curry School of Education, University of Virginia

Cheryl Keenan, Director of Adult Education, State of Pennsylvania

Myrna Manley, Retired Teacher and Author, El Camino College

Joanne Meier, Assistant Professor, Curry School of Education, University of Virginia

Donna Miller-Parker, Director of Essential Skills Programs, Shoreline Community College, Seattle, Washington

Mark Moody, Assistant Superintendent for Planning, Results, and Information Management, Maryland Department of Education

Pamela A. Moss, Associate Professor, School of Education, University of Michigan

Mari Pearlman, Vice President, Division of Teaching and Learning, Educational Testing Service

Barbara S. Plake, W.C. Meierhenry Distinguished Professor of Educational Psychology and Director of the Oscar and Luella Buros Center for Testing, University of Nebraska at Lincoln

Mark D. Reckase, Professor of Measurement and Quantitative Methods, Department of Counseling, Educational Psychology, and Special Education, Michigan State University

Stephen G. Sireci, Associate Professor, School of Education, University of Massachusetts at Amherst
Sondra Stein, Senior Research Associate, National Institute for Literacy
David Thissen, Professor of Psychology, University of North Carolina at Chapel Hill
Fran Tracy-Mumford, State Supervisor for Adult and Community Education, Delaware Department of Public Instruction
Katherine (Kit) A. Viator, Administrator for Student Testing, Massachusetts Department of Education
Wendy M. Yen, Vice President of Research at K-12 Works, Educational Testing Service

Guests

Sandra Baxter, National Institute for Literacy
Brenda Bell, Center for Literacy Studies, University of Tennessee
Martha Berlin, Westat
Sue Bowers, U.S. Department of Education
Osa Brand, Association of American Geographers
Joyce Campbell, U.S. Department of Education
Alicia Cascallar, Federation of State Boards of Physical Therapy
Larry Condelli, American Institutes for Research
Anna Critz, ACT, Inc.
Carol D'Amico, U.S. Department of Education
Denise Daniels, District of Columbia Public Schools
Daria Ellis, National Board for Professional Teaching Standards
Penelope Engel, Educational Testing Service
Michael Fong, U.S. Department of Education
Carol Fuller, National Association of Independent Colleges and Universities
Brenda Gagne, Maine Department of Education
Elaine Gilby, U.S. Department of Education
Marilyn Gillespie, SRI International
Lynda Ginsburg, National Center on Adult Literacy, University of Pennsylvania
Barbara Goodwin, Maine Department of Education
Sharon Healy, Maryland Department of Education
Eugene Johnson, American Institutes for Research
Michael Jones, U.S. Department of Education

Dorry Kenyon, Center for Applied Linguistics
Andrew Kolstad, U.S. Department of Education
Kristen Kulongoski, Oregon Department of Community Colleges
Mark Kutner, American Institutes for Research
Mariann Lemke, U.S. Department of Education
Mohammed Louguit, Center for Applied Linguistics
Mary Lovell, U.S. Department of Education
Christopher Mazzeo, National Governors Association
Peggy McGuire, National Institute for Literacy
Lennox McLendon, National Adult Education/Professional Development Consortium
Rebecca Moak, U.S. Department of Education
Leyla Mohadjer, Westat
Pat Montalvan, Westat
Sarah Newcomb, U.S. Department of Education
James Parker, U.S. Department of Education
Robert Pasternack, U.S. Department of Education
Kathleen Petrek, National Institute for Literacy
Loretta Petty, U.S. Department of Education
Ron Pugsley, U.S. Department of Education
Sen Qi, American Council on Education
Lynn Reese, Center on Education and Training for Employment, Ohio State University
Laura Roach, Oregon Department of Community Colleges
John Sabatini, National Center on Adult Literacy, University of Pennsylvania
Tanya Shuy, National Institutes of Health
Stephanie Stauffer, Center for Applied Linguistics
Shirley Steele, U.S. Department of Education
Regie Stites, SRI International
Carol Van Duzer, National Center for ESL Literacy Education
Nicole Vartanian, U.S. Department of Education
Sheida White, U.S. Department of Education
Jean Yan, Westat
Cindy Zengler, Ohio Department of Education

NRC Staff

Pasquale DeVito, Director, Board on Testing and Assessment
Michael Feuer, Director, Center for Education
Kaeli Knowles, Board on Testing and Assessment
Judith Koenig, Board on Testing and Assessment
Patricia Morison, Center for Education
Nevzer Stacey, Center for Education
Andrew Tompkins, Board on Testing and Assessment

APPENDIX

C
Adult Education and Family Literacy Act FY 2001 Appropriation for State Grants

STATE	ALLOCATION
ALABAMA	$9,461,502
ALASKA	753,679
ARIZONA	5,950,133
ARKANSAS	5,660,506
CALIFORNIA	52,665,928
COLORADO	3,948,986
CONNECTICUT	5,208,229
DELAWARE	1,307,077
FLORIDA	25,258,267
GEORGIA	13,335,195
HAWAII	1,753,520
IDAHO	1,611,540
ILLINOIS	19,313,949
INDIANA	9,610,644
IOWA	3,990,564
KANSAS	3,452,210
KENTUCKY	9,194,809
LOUISIANA	9,156,449
MAINE	2,069,917
MARYLAND	7,675,347
MASSACHUSETTS	8,933,714

STATE	ALLOCATION
MICHIGAN	15,159,503
MINNESOTA	5,459,810
MISSISSIPPI	6,258,511
MISSOURI	9,546,350
MONTANA	1,289,909
NEBRASKA	2,179,764
NEVADA	2,175,779
NEW HAMPSHIRE	1,669,046
NEW JERSEY	13,284,133
NEW MEXICO	2,808,908
NEW YORK	32,730,637
NORTH CAROLINA	14,190,851
NORTH DAKOTA	1,204,609
OHIO	18,467,796
OKLAHOMA	5,760,948
OREGON	4,124,840
PENNSYLVANIA	21,509,189
RHODE ISLAND	2,253,258
SOUTH CAROLINA	7,765,616
SOUTH DAKOTA	1,298,537
TENNESSEE	11,511,054
TEXAS	32,712,918
UTAH	1,832,021
VERMONT	1,001,079
VIRGINIA	11,065,506
WASHINGTON	5,991,395
WEST VIRGINIA	4,507,500
WISCONSIN	7,347,252
WYOMING	761,550
DISTRICT OF COLUMBIA	1,489,139
PUERTO RICO	11,274,054
VIRGIN ISLANDS	218,832
AMERICAN SAMOA	208,468
GUAM	313,376
NO. MARIANA IS.	375,103
MARSHALL IS.	72,900

STATE	ALLOCATION
MICRONESIA	72,900
PALAU	72,900
Total, State Grants	**$460,278,106**
PREL Competitive Grant Set-aside	81,294
Incentive Grants Set-aside	9,640,600
TOTAL	**$470,000,000**